The Book of DH

MONUMENTAL PRAISE FOR THE BOOK OF DH

"Since our days at Michigan Business School, I have marveled at Damon's ability to pivot his career and personal life. It is amazing how a kid from South Central LA would have stories about Shanghai, Rome, Rio de Janeiro, Barcelona and throughout the USA. He's worked with the most popular brands and athletes in the world. I love his mind, his grind, and his heart! If nothing else, *The Book of DH* will be a testament to the truth...all is possible!"

Ron Chandler
Leader, US Education
Apple

"You can never underestimate the heart and determination of a champion and one that overcomes incredible odds. Damon and I grew up on the same block and attended the same high school. We are family. We knew one another before the world knew us. Movies and television shows are created based on a life we once lived. *The Book of DH* is a true story about an unlikely path through the hood, Corporate America and entrepreneurship. And more importantly, what it takes to create the path and pave the way."

Wendy Raquel Robinson
Actress of CW's *The Game*

"Amazing and flawless describes the work Damon and his teams produced from creative to execution for the HBO Brand. We have remained friends over the years and I have been able to see his journey firsthand. Woven within his personal story are thought-provoking ideas and concepts that are sure to inspire, inform and ignite your thinking to help you better navigate your path to success."

Maria Weaver
President, WMX
@Warner Music Group

MONUMENTAL PRAISE FOR THE BOOK OF DH

"The Book of DH represents the passion and wisdom of a trusted mentor and friend who inspired me to step beyond my comfort zone. I forever quote Damon's advice that I needed to trust myself and realize that I was more than "the job title and company on my business card!" Much gratitude for Damon's presence and power to connect people with their purpose."

Janiece Evans-Page
CEO Tides

"Championship drive is the phrase that best describes Damon Haley. Starting with our early days of developing one of the largest youth sports leagues in the Los Angeles market, the Nike/YMCA Jr Lakers League, to working on community activations with some of the most dynamic athletes in the world, Damon has time and again proven that he is a savant when it comes to the sports marketing game. More importantly, to me, he does it with a voice and flair that represents us."

Erikk Aldridge
AEG, Vice President, Community Affairs
Founder of the Inglewood Baseball Fund

"Through my rise with Nike and Jordan Brand and now as a CEO, Damon has always been a valued thought partner, voice of reason and driving force. His range of experiences and situational encounters is extraordinary. More so, his willingness to share and impact the lives of young professionals and entrepreneurs is unmatched. Anyone striving to reach their personal 'next level' is sure to use *The Book of DH* as a stepping stone."

Chad Easterling
Co-Founder / CEO
Obsidianworks Media & Marketing Agency

"Damon is the big brother to LA basketball culture. As a kid, there were very few positive Black executives coming from the hood and helping out kids and programs that didn't have the resources. He pioneered Basketball and Community and we are all products of his hard work, dedication and vision. True role model and someone I will always look up to."

Baron Davis
Former NBA Player
Tech Entrepreneur

MONUMENTAL PRAISE FOR THE BOOK OF DH

"Damon made me feel brave. He was an African American leader at Nike who brought his authentic self to work at a time when it was not popular for Black people to do so at the brand. He possesses the unique quality of owning the room while making everyone in it feel valued and respected."

Nicol Thomas
Former Nike Marketing Executive

"I have coached many people in my life, very powerful people in politics and business. So, I can say I don't get easily impressed. I met Damon, not knowing anything about him when I was conducting a training where he was a participant. I found myself hanging on every word this man uttered. His wisdom, depth, and righteous spirit made an indelible mark on me. I believe you are up for a great treat reading his book. For sure it will be a journey of growth."

Alberto Botero
Transformational Trainer and Coach, Author of *Thinking In Images*

"Damon's mentality is always: Stay hungry and humble. Never be at ease. Even if you're number one in your industry, act like you are number three."

Jason Cohn
North America Events Lead
Apple

"I was concerned about leaving Nike and the lack of security a new opportunity presented. When Damon said there's no security at Nike, I left and never regretted it."

Jerry Sawyer
Chief of Staff
Kobe Bryant Inc.

"Damon is one of the smartest people I know and one of the most thoughtful. He goes hard in everything he pursues and I'm honored to call him a friend and mentor."

Mike Parker
Head of Lifestyle & Fashion
Reebok

The Book of DH

Tightroping the Systems, Breakthroughs and Triumphs

Damon Haley

Edited by Angela Benson & Kai Adia

Bee Infinite Publishing

Copyright © 2022 by Damon Haley

All rights reserved. No part of this book may be reproduced in any manner whatsoever without written permission except in the case of brief quotations embodied in critical articles and reviews.

First Printing, 2022

CONTENTS

	A TIMELINE OF DAMON HALEY'S LIFE AND CAREER	xi
	DEDICATION	xv
	INTRODUCTION	xvii
1	Getting Punched in the Mouth	1
2	A Monster Stole the Fear	7
3	Rosa was on to Something	17
4	Look to the Left, Look to the Right	28
5	Wrong Time. Wrong Situation. Wrong Guy.	43
6	The Swoosh Life	65
7	The U	85
8	Mr. International	104
9	Nothing Lasts Forever	117
10	Hold Up, the Party is Not Over	133
	MY DAD AND ME	141
	CHAPTER TAKEAWAYS	157

| ix |

> "Dang!" You thought you'd be living large by this time. The professionals are supposed to live long and prosper. You've gone astray, —Dom

LIL DH IN THE MAKING

A TIMELINE OF DAMON HALEY'S LIFE AND CAREER

1966 -1984

- Born and raised in South Central Los Angeles (1966 - 1984)
- Begins busing to school (1973)
- Graduates from George Washington Preparatory High School (1984)

1984 - 1989

- 1984
    - Summer Olympics in Los Angeles
    - Begins college at Cal Berkeley
- 1985
    - Becomes a Phi Beta Sigma Man
    - Cal Berkeley Baseball Team try-outs
    - Becomes a lab assistant for Cal Berkeley Child Development Program
- 1986
    - Declares Economics as a college major
- 1989
    - Graduates from Cal Berkeley
    - Accepts a position at Occidental College
    - Serves as a Camera Operator and Show Producer for Continental Cable

1990 - 1992

- Begins MBA Program at University of Michigan (1990)
- Interns with University of Michigan Athletics Department (1991)
    - Desmond Howard wins Heisman Trophy
    - Fab 5 reaches Final Four and Championship Game
- Interns with Chevron Corporation (1991)

A TIMELINE OF DAMON HALEY'S LIFE AND CAREER

- Graduates from the University of Michigan and accepts a position with Chevron (1992)

1993 - 1995

- Holds positions in Chevron's Treasury, Shipping, Overseas, Corporate Strategy and Pension Fund Management Groups
- Serves as Business Manager for Righteous Records and Consultant to Phunky Phat Graphix
- Board of Director Member of San Francisco National Black MBA Association and Oakland Phi Beta Sigma Graduate Chapter

1996 - 1999

- Resigns from Chevron and becomes Head of Marketing for Nike Western Region
    - Major League Soccer Deal // Galaxy (1996 - 1999)
    - Olympics Activation Management Team (1996)
    - 5 Nike Towns Launch in Los Angeles, Seattle, San Francisco, Las Vegas and Hawaii (1997 - 1999)
    - California Interscholastic Federation Southern Section High School Championship Deal (1997 - 1999)
    - Magic Johnson's Midsummer Night's Deal (1997 - 1999)
    - Jordan Brand Launch (1997)
    - WNBA Deal // Sparks (1997 - 1998)
    - NFL Licensing Deal // Raiders, Cowboys, Broncos (1998 - 1999)
    - NBA Licensing Deal // Lakers, Blazers (1998 - 1999)

2000 - 2012

- Resigns from Nike and launches UMCA Sports & Entertainment Company
    - First UMCA project: Warner Bros Theatrical Release of the movie *Bait* starring Jamie Foxx (2000)
    - Allen Iverson NBA All-Star Weekend // Oakland (2000)
    - Kobe Bryant Adidas Shoe Launch // Nationwide (2000)
    - Michael Jordan Flight Academy (2000 - 2010)
    - HBO Marketing Consultancy (2001 - 2008)
    - Michael Jordan Senior Flight School (2001 - 2010)
    - Sega NBA 2K Celebrity Tournament at NBA All-Star Weekend - Washington, D.C. (2001) and Philadelphia (2002)

A TIMELINE OF DAMON HALEY'S LIFE AND CAREER

- Paramount Pictures Marketing Consultancy (2002 - 2007)
- Nike NBA All-Star Weekend Activation (2003 - 2016)
- LeBron James First Shoe Release (2003)
- Nike Assignment // Kobe Bryant (2003)
- Jordan Brand NBA All-Star Activation // Los Angeles & Las Vegas (2004 & 2007)
- Michael Vick Shoe Launch (2004 - 2006)
- Jordan Brand Breakfast Club (2004 - 2008)
- Kobe Bryant First Nike Shoe Launch - Huarache (2005)
- Nickelodeon Marketing Consultancy (2004 - 2010)
- Tyler Perry / Lionsgate Marketing Consultancy (2005 - 2008)
- Frito Lay Marketing Consultancy (2006 - 2008)
- Gatorade Marketing Consultancy (2007)
- Final Four Nike Activation // San Antonio (2008)
- Pepsi North America Marketing Consultancy (2008 - 2010)
- LeBron James King's Academy (2006)
- Kobe Bryant Academy (2007 - 2014)
- Converse Shoe Athlete Marketing (2010)
- Cartoon Network Marketing Consultancy (2010 - 2012)
- Festival of Sport // Shanghai (2011 - 2012)
- NFL China Launch // Shanghai (2012)
- Final Four Nike Activation // New Orleans (2012)

2013 - 2018

- Divests from UMCA. Engages in independent consulting projects
  - Nike Batalas Das Quadras // Rio De Janiero & Sao Paulo (2013)
  - Nike Greater China 'Come Out & Play' Campaign // Shanghai (2013)
- Becomes Troika Media Group Sports Account Director - Deals (2013)
  - Charlotte Hornets
  - Jacksonville Jaguars
  - Ultimate Fighting Championship
  - Red Bull
- Resigns from Troika to Engage in independent consulting projects (2014 - 2018)
  - Nike World Basketball Festival (2014)
  - Kobe Bryant / TZ Sports Gaming Partnership (2014 - 2015)
  - Kobe Bryant Muse (2015)
  - Hennessy 250 Year Anniversary (2015)
  - Jordan 30 Year Anniversary // Greater China (2015)
  - Nike Global Basketball Consultancy (2015 - 2016)
  - NBA All-Star Weekend // Toronto (2016)

| xiii |

A TIMELINE OF DAMON HALEY'S LIFE AND CAREER

- ◦ DME Sports Academy Marketing Consultancy // Daytona Beach, FL (2017)
- Becomes Troika Head of Sports Marketing (2017 - 2018)

2019 - Present

- Forms Haley Beauty Holdings and purchases two beauty businesses (2019)
- Acquires Equity Stake in the 'Hoop Dreams' Trademark (2021)
- Forms Phenom Consulting Group (2021)

DEDICATION

The Book of DH is dedicated to everyone that never had a chance to get a chance, those that were worthy of a chance but were denied a chance, and anyone who straight up took the chance and defeated incredible odds to succeed.

We all are striving to go from nothing to just being good, from good to great, and from great to phenomenal. Ascending to great heights is not an easy feat, but the value and power is in the courage to take the journey. Know that you are not alone and that I am right there with you. I want you to succeed at whatever your quest is... just have one, or many.

It is vital to develop a self-winning formula that fits your style and flow. You will be faced with getting punched in the mouth, encounter individuals and systems that try to intimidate you, and even unfair barriers and obstacles set forth and enabled by privilege. Despite all of that, you can and will achieve. Don't stop. Won't stop. Your triumph and success is always within your grasp.

This book is not just about me, it's about all those who 'knew me back when'. I dedicate this book to my block and my neighborhood. You know who you are. If we spent time at school, church or at the park together, I am speaking to you. If you lived or worked in the 90047 zip code or your people do, thank you for everything. Your presence and impact in my life mattered. If you knew my parents and siblings and showed me love, I appreciate you. I have nothing but love for all of my play uncles, aunts, brothers and sisters on 84th Place. I know first hand how tough and rough it was in our hood. But, no matter what, we were a community. Black men were present in the

DEDICATION

home, working and leading families. Kids were playing in the streets and enjoying life. Mommas were being mommas to all of us. We had some characters in the hood who were wild and misguided. We also had a few young brothas that gave South Central a bad and horrific reputation. And then there were some of us that were misunderstood. We loved them all. They were us and we were them. Know that I take you wherever I go and you are in all that I do. I love you.

I dedicate this book to my awesome family: my mom, my last living big brother Eric, and my one and only sister Elaine. Please keep supporting, pushing and loving me. I was lucky to be the baby and to have so many protectors, role models and instructors. You made family, home and street life easy for me. A special shout out to the Shinns, Bryants, Craigs, Williams, Mathews, Deveareauxs, Valentines, Gabriels and Dunns and the rest of my family tree. We are a brilliant, radiant, phenomenal family. Our roots run deep and our blood is strong. Let's keep uplifting one another. Our greatness is in our future.

I want to give a special dedication to the men who are no longer with me. Thank you to my big brother Alvin who I was able to have a strong relationship with when we both grew and became men. To my brother Fatty, you were my hero, villain, friend and my everything. I am still trying to outwit, out funny, and out do you. I appreciate all the nudges to build my character. And then there is the big guy, my dad. He is the G.O.A.T of a dad. You gave me everything I needed. You gave me the right fuel for my mission and I cannot wait until I see you again. I got stories for you.

Last but not least, I want to thank my wife Diann for giving me the vision to create the unthinkable. Thanks for the constant inspiration through your actions and aspirations for a phenomenal life. You have injected me with your quest for excellence, energy to go higher and a keen sense of humility. Love you to the moon and back, and even more. Ride or die, baby!

INTRODUCTION

BY DIANN VALENTINE

If you know Damon Haley, then you probably believe in Dreams & Hopes, Baby! His visionary approach to life, his passion, and undying enthusiasm are contagious...and sometimes overwhelming. Damon and I met in Oakland, CA when he was a Financial Analyst at Chevron and I was an up-and-coming entrepreneur and wedding designer. While at Chevron, Damon was consulting and serving as a business manager to a few Bay Area businesses. One of his clients and one of my vendors was Thomas Underwood of Phunky Phat Graphix– the creative engine around Bay Area Hip Hop icons such as Too Short, E-40, and Master P to name a few. Thomas encouraged Damon to create a relationship with me and to look at my wedding conference called African American Brides of Distinction, which was one of the first of its kind. Damon attended the conference and we talked briefly. Flash forward a few years later, I found myself sitting across from Damon in a Nike conference room as he had transitioned to launch the Nike Western Region Marketing Group.

We exchanged contact information and I shared with him that the trajectory of my career was changing and ultimately led to my move to Los Angeles. I was producing my biggest project to date which was actress Lela Rochon and movie director Antoine Fuqua's wedding. I had the wedding handled but I needed to figure out how to leverage my relationship with the Moet & Chandon representative I had incorporated into the wedding celebration. At the wedding reception, I sat Damon

INTRODUCTION

next to the Moet representative. The result? He sparked a multi-year, multi-million dollar relationship with my company and Moet! After that, Damon and I remained respected colleagues. As my career skyrocketed in Los Angeles, he was always available to offer a great business perspective and a listening ear without any agenda, unlike most men I had encountered in entertainment. When he launched UMCA Sports & Entertainment, I became UMCA's lead Event Producer.

Personally, Damon and I became good friends. He became my 'marketing guy' with my corporate clients, as I became his go-to event producer. I was a single mother in a new city and did not have an extensive network of friends and trusted confidantes. I was fearless and believed I could 'have it all' but I needed a 'Damon Haley' in my life. Oftentimes, Damon would pick up my daughter Riann from school and drop her off at home. He would even show up to her Saturday morning swim meets and high school basketball games. Damon understood that I had the highest aspirations to be the best in the wedding and luxury lifestyle space and he did everything he could to advance, elevate and support me. Whether it was stepping in to give my daughter a ride, wowing a marketing executive, or leading the security detail at one of my events, Damon was always supportive of me and my journey. That is what the Dreams & Hopes part of him is all about...helping, supporting, assisting, driving, and motivating others.

As our relationship grew, our friendship transitioned into L-O-V-E. Ultimately, I married my best friend and the most supportive man I'd met since my Dad. He was a gentle and kind spirit, a positive influence in my daughter's life, and the business partner I always longed for. We were equally driven entrepreneurs–me as a designer, producer, author, speaker, and TV host. On the other hand, Damon was a highly sought-after marketing talent and strategic thought partner for global brands and icons. Regardless of who led the project–if it was a Nike, HBO, LeBron James, Moet Hennessy, TD Jakes, Pepsi, or Los Angeles Lakers project–we maintained our Diann Valentine and Damon Haley identities while delivering best in class work, service and results. We did all this while still enjoying each other along the way.

It has truly been so inspiring to see Damon transition from a 'numbers guy' at Chevron to a 'marketing guy' at Nike, to an accomplished business owner with UMCA, to a strategy consultant for global brands and icons, to now leading our family's beauty businesses. And yes, this global sports marketing guy who has rubbed elbows with Michael Jordan, Kobe Bryant, and LeBron James and has led countless macho, highly competitive and high testosterone men is driving a beauty business! He has been able to bundle all of his knowledge and apply it to each step during his journey, making each move better than the last. He is really smart, quick, intuitive and an overall visionary.

Damon understands concepts, ideas, mapping, plans and programs much faster than the average person regardless of whether he is in North or South America, Asia, Africa or Europe—which continues to fascinate me. I have seen DH Baby mesmerize audiences, shift the decisions of high-level executives, influence consumer purchasing decisions and still manage to understand the hearts and souls of consumers across the world regardless of ethnicity, language barriers or cultural differences. "DH Baby " is his magic. Pardon me, his DH Baobei (Greater China) / Dahzinho (Brazil) / DH Tesoro (Italy) / Gbujan (Sierra Leone) / DH Baby thing across the world. And even more impressive, Damon is straight up 'South Central' and most people do not immediately think he is a Cal Berkeley graduate and has an MBA from Michigan. He gives everyone from the youngster on the street to the C-Suite executive the same respect, care, consideration and 'push-push, drive-drive' energy to achieve and be their best selves professionally and personally. I have seen Damon navigate the CMOs and VPs at brands such as Nike, Sony, Time Warner, Viacom, Coca Cola and others with wonderment. He builds 'buy in', supreme trust, and hype on humongous, risky projects like only he can do. Companies trusted Damon all the way to success and new heights. I am the proudest wife on the planet as I reflect on

INTRODUCTION

what UMCA, my company Exhilarate Experiential and Damon have accomplished.

With great strides in life as well as the pursuit and the accomplishment of great things, there is a concept always prevalent in Damon and even within his victory. That concept is 'The Gap'. The Gap is the element that is the difference between 100% and where you landed if you did not crush 'it' at 100%. Ever since I have known Damon, he has been about HIS 100%. Obsessed with it sometimes? Completely. Neurotic about it sometimes? Absolutely. Overboard? Always. All of the above and then some about 100% and The Gap? Frantically! With that said, he has always had a method and uncontrollable energy to rally people to rise to THEIR 100% when working or engaging with him. Damon has a way of willing people to do their best which pushes them in ways they have never been pushed before. He's able to find that area in one's brain and heart that wakes up the need for excellence, not just for a moment in time but essentially as a reboot of one's life, shifting their perspective and changing their trajectory. Whether you like it, love it, hate it, or run from it, Damon always seems to get people thinking about The Gap. Damon is a winner and he changes people who are around him to win and win big. He finds a way to set a path of new standards with everyone he engages. *The Book of DH* will challenge and invite you to examine your standards and 'The Gaps' in your life but more importantly, receive the tips and insight to bridge those gaps, aim higher, intensify your focus and create the life you've always dreamed of regardless of what you are faced with.

As Damon shares his journey, he will reveal his peaks, valleys, pitfalls and obstacles along the way. As a brilliant Black man striving to succeed in the United States of America, predominately white educational institutions, and Corporate America, you can imagine a myriad of challenges that he faced...and is still facing. Being Black in America comes with the expected nuances of racism and discrimination. Now amplify that with being raised in South Central Los Angeles, enrolled in the most prestigious universities, working for multinational companies,

INTRODUCTION

and serving brands and athletes who are #1 in their respective fields. His stories and experiences are extraordinary. I am proud that Damon created the time to write *The Book of DH* as a way to share not only his life, but also his personal accounts of happenings along the way.

Many of us read headlines, biographies, resumes and scroll through social media and LinkedIn profiles, only to assume that such information is someone's entire story. Damon's story is complex and remarkable. In *The Book of DH*, Damon shares his truths about how the odds are stacked against some and favorable to others as well as how to persevere, pivot, progress and, most of all, keep your dream alive. When it comes to his brilliance, my husband is a humble man. He is the smartest man I know. He will never take enough credit for building the Nike Brand in the United States of America and connecting it to the rise of Hip Hop. Nor will he take enough credit for sparking Nike's ascend to great heights in Greater China. I will scream it loudly from the rooftops because I saw it first-hand. He will not willingly talk about the numerous brands and people his strategic thinking elevated during his stint as Managing Partner of UMCA. I will. He will not take credit for being Nike's go-to thought leader and making things happen when the company signed LeBron James and Kobe Bryant because they didn't understand Black people and Black culture. I will. What Damon does in *The Book of DH* is provide context and he shares relevant tips on pushing toward any glass ceiling. He shows how to compete career-wise at the highest level. He'll share insight on what it takes to build your business with Corporate America or with athletes and entertainers. Why? Because you must hold on tight to your dreams and hopes like your life depends on it, because it does. You must understand the dynamics in play with respect to the systems, privilege and 'isms' and how that affects your chances, opportunities, and advancement. Some things are tough to describe, and many people will not convey the truth of their experiences...the good, bad and ugly. Damon shares it all so that you will succeed and exceed his trajectory in life.

The Book of DH is real talk if you are ready for it. DH Baby!

1

Getting Punched in the Mouth

> *It's funny like that in the hood sometimes. You never knew what was gonna happen.*
>
> CAINE, MENACE II SOCIETY

Do you remember the first time someone hit you? Do you remember as a kid play-fighting in the sandbox or rough-housing with your neighbor in the backyard? Think back to the first time someone tried to inflict bodily harm on you. Or, maybe the first time you got your ass whipped by someone other than your mom, dad, or siblings. How did you respond? There is a reaction theory of freeze, flight, or fight. The theory, in a nutshell, is: did you do nothing, did you run, or did you fight? Depending on your recollection, your first reaction could have been a learned behavior or an instinct. If you are playing the game of life and all its splendor, you are bound to get punched in the mouth a few times. If you stand up for yourself, for other people or causes, someone or an entity will try to punch you in the mouth, or even try to kill you. And sometimes, you can be in the wrong place at the wrong time and get punched for no reason. So in essence, the punch is coming. The most important variable is how you respond to the punch and how you feel about possibly getting pushed around for the rest of your life.

The first time I can recall getting punched in the mouth made me see the world in a totally different way. A huge part of my early years was hanging out with my brothers, spending time on my block, and playing with the kids in the neighborhood. Growing up in the 70s, we didn't have video games and today's technology, so most tweens and teens spent all of their time outdoors at one another's houses or simply 'in the streets' until the streetlights came on. My brother Fatty was a deviant, even at a young age. He was also the prototypical big brother. He was my bully, friend, enemy and all that comes with older siblings. One day, he arranged a fight for me. The challenger was a friend of mine, Delano. To this day, Delano and I are still friends and I consider him a brother. I will always remember Delano delivering the first deadly blow I had ever received in life. His family grew up on our block and our family members were inseparable–going to school together, hanging out and having fun on the regular.

Fatty just popped up and said, "Hey, you're going to fight Delano." And I was thinking, "We are friends. Why would I? That's my guy, my dude." Delano was a smaller guy but he was tough and had a big heart. I was truly perplexed about the fight. I didn't understand it but I can still tap into what I felt then. I was not in fear, but I simply did not understand the purpose. In the moment, I wasn't even focused on winning, I was more perplexed by the fight. The match was in Delano's backyard. There was a lot of chatter and instigating because there were so many youngsters in our neighborhood who had made their way to Delano's backyard. Younger brothers' fighting was entertaining to the older siblings.

Delano was already positioned on the backyard porch of his house when I got there. The porch had about eight steps. Delano was on the top step and I was on the bottom step. My gut told me that Delano didn't want to fight me either, but there was a point where it felt like a Mexican standoff. I relaxed and took my eye off Delano for one split second, and that dude ran down the steps and knocked the crap out of me! Then, he ran right back up the steps. It was not a lightweight blow or a knockout punch, but it shook, stunned, and mesmerized me. Delano remained cool and unaffected. He looked the same as he did before he punched me in the mouth. He didn't antagonize, taunt or provoke me, but Delano also did not have a look of sorrow, forgiveness, empathy, or the like on his face. His look and body language said, "I made my move, what are you going to do?" Despite encouragement from the crowd that formed, I didn't attack or fight Delano. Only my feelings were hurt, but that was about it. And honestly, I was not then, nor am I the type of guy to put on a show for others' entertainment. I simply told my brother I wanted to go home. After some not so kind words from my big brother Fatty, we went home. The next day, Delano and I were back to being friends.

Be Aware and Anticipate the Punch

Every time I see Delano, the first thing I think about is that smack in the face... that first punch in the mouth. It taught me in this world you have to keep your head on a swivel and to be aware at all times. Due to that early encounter, I was prepared to never be at ease because the situation, environment or people can change at a moment's notice. You just simply have to be prepared for obstacles and disappointments, it's part of the game. Once you're prepared, you won't be surprised.

Growing up in South Central Los Angeles, I have dealt with so many characters–some good, some bad. I have lived through the struggles of the 70s, the 80s, the LAPD, and the crack epidemic. Fortunately, I did not receive more punches in the mouth literally, but I did figuratively. Smacks in the mouth were just a way of life in South Central. The real question is, how do you deal with it? My oldest brother, Alvin, passed away recently. Alvin was a drug addict in his 20s. PCP, Angel Dust and Sherm smacked him in the mouth early in his adult life and he could not overcome the addiction or turn the corner. Alvin died never being able to rebound from the fight. For some reason, he could not shake the drug he consumed and experienced in the 70s nor recover from it 50 years later. I lost a good friend named Eddie recently as well. Early in his life, he couldn't fight his demons, so he turned to alcohol and eventually developed kidney cancer. At age 55, Eddie admitted that his alcoholism just caught up with him. Alvin and Eddie died within a week of one another.

This marked a tough time for me as the Grim Reaper hit me with a one-two punch within 7 days. I lost my big brother Fatty a few years back at age 55...another double nickel death. He was a hustler for most of his adult life and could not shake the vice grip the South Central streets had on him. Later, when I grew up, I had the means and ways to help my big brother change his life. I flipped the script and organized 'bouts' for him in the form of skill training, job interviews, project work, etc. Fatty never responded to the challenge. His opponent, the fight, was too much for him. He lived and endured a rough life before he succumbed to lung cancer.

Living through physical, mental, and emotional despair taught me that when I encounter a punch in the mouth, I must respond accordingly. I know it's going to happen. I've been in many 'boxing matches and fights' throughout my life. Yet, my reaction to it has always been, "Okay, I'm going to fight through this, I'm going to figure it out." This style of living was and is painful at times, but I swear to God I never ever took my eye off of an opponent of any sort after getting smacked up by Delano. My journey has always been about protecting myself first, fighting back second, and assessing if fighting back is even necessary.

Moving Through Chaos

I was reading the other day about Rockefeller's wealth. A question was posed with respect to how do you become wealthy? A vital and critical part of it is protecting your assets and, of course, making money and then being your own bank. But then, there was this protection scenario involved. So I always think part of the getting-punched-in-the-mouth phase is how are you going about protecting assets before, during, and after the punch? How are you seeing the things that are happening around you so that you can respond accordingly?

There is another philosophical perspective I believe in by Nassim Nicholas Taleb. He wrote a bunch of books. He's a mathematician and a hedge fund guy. He has a book called *Antifragile: Things That Gain from Disorder*. His concept of antifragility consists of: how do you succeed when there is chaos? If you are fragile, you break. If you concentrate on antifragility, how do you prosper? One must be fluid, lucid, nimble, flexible and you must have the mentality, will, and temperament to build the skills to do so.

My boy Delano was not ready for our fight. He did not prepare. He just hit me. He got his lick in, and he was not hit. On the other hand, I was hit, beat, and confused. If there was an event that shaped my life, that moment was it. I don't call it a sucker punch because if you are in a fight, hey, you're the sucker if you get punched first. Or, if you are out there in the world, there is no such thing as a sucker punch. 'Punches' are looking for suckers. Be on the lookout for the punch. And, it is cool to get punched. If you are not getting punched every now and then, you are not going up against worthy opponents in life or you are not pushing yourself to breakthrough the limits that may surround you. To advance, progress, and achieve all things that define triumph, you must embrace and come out on the other side as a winner when you take those punches.

Key Takeaways

- Maintain the mindset to compete at all times. Not fight, per se, but always be ready to 'flip the switch' if necessary.

- Others may 'negotiate' fights and conflict for you. Don't fall into those traps. Pick your own battles and wars.

- Don't think too long and hard over punches, fights and losses. Stuff happens. Learn and move on.

2

A Monster Stole the Fear

> *You cannot fear anything. Fear is what stops you and makes you weak. It makes your mental constructs feeble.*
> THAAL SINESTRO, GREEN LANTERN

The time was the 1980s and the place was South Central Los Angeles. I grew up in a Crip neighborhood. The gang set was Eight Tray Gangster Crips. They were one of the biggest and most notorious gangs with many alliances and rivals. Their biggest rival was the Rollin' 60s Crips. Although I lived, went to school, and played in the 'war zone', I never had an interest or appetite for gangbanging. I didn't really believe in it, and I did not succumb to it. However, I did understand it. It was a way of life in my neighborhood for some, and a perceived best option to fight the many challenges we faced. There were many predators and bad dudes who used membership in gangs just to survive or prey on people in the hood versus fighting the bigger societal enemies. But, there were some real OGs that for whatever reason would die for 'the set' and would treat enemies how racist individuals treat Black folks in this country. There was one OG in particular, who will remain nameless, that at the time was the biggest and baddest guy in the neighborhood. To me, it meant he was the baddest guy in the world. We would hear stories of him 'putting hands' on people, beating people, shooting people and I witnessed the day he miraculously escaped death when caught by a rival gang with seemingly no way out. He was, without question, legendary.

No Need to Fear Any Man, Any Situation, Any Circumstance

In my younger years, there was no internet, social media, mobile phones, etc. Word of mouth was the way news went viral, per se. One day, I was not in school. I had a dental or medical appointment so I was out of the loop of information. My appointment was extended until the afternoon, so my pops dropped me off a block away from the park. I grabbed some fries from the local burger joint and headed to the park. My usual day-to-day route was to take a back entrance through an alley and then a hole through a chain link fence. I did not get the word that on this day, there would be a gang meeting at the park. This was the era of drive-by shootings, random beat downs, and chaos in the streets when there was a gang meeting. You would just have to sprint home from school and stay in the house because your life depended on it. You would not want to be caught on the streets at the wrong time because these gangbangers would be high or drunk and looking for prey to pounce on. The gangbangers would just roll up on you for no apparent reason because this is the kind of culture many of us grew up in.

I found myself going through the chain link fence, and before I realized it I had just walked in on a full-fledged gang meeting. That was a big problem, and the biggest I had ever faced up to this point. I was not in their gang, a rival gang, or any gang at all. I felt death as all eyes turned on me. These gangbangers typically mutilated, shot and beat people for sport. That is simply how it worked. Miraculously, I did not panic, and there was no escape anyway. My 'wheels' were not fast enough to outrun the gang to freedom. Plus, if they wanted to hunt me later, it would have been easy to find out where I lived, catch me in the streets, or find me at school. Plus, my dad always said the minute you run and show your ass, you are the prey. I saw the leader of the gang—the biggest, baddest man on the planet—close by. I made a beeline right to him. He was my only chance to survive. I said, "Hey, I just want to go home." I knew I was not supposed to be there and he knew it too. In the background, I heard so much chatter. "What up, cuz? What up? Beat his ass. What up, blood? What set you from?" There were so many gangsters around me just waiting to see how the OG would respond. I repeated, as calmly as I could, "I just want to go home." I didn't try to explain or answer any questions because pleading could have been more dangerous.

There were enough people standing around who knew me from the neighborhood. They either went to school with me, knew me from the park or the block, but none of this mattered. The game was weird like that. Everything from group-think to independence was part of the game, and gang mentality and scenarios like this held the community hostage. At this point, I was just sport and I knew it. It seemed like an eternity for the OG to say anything. Anything at all. Then suddenly, two people I knew, Arthur and Spanky, said, "Stall him out," which basically meant "give him a pass." Everybody else was staring at me like I was fresh meat. Back then, the drink of choice was Olde English 800 and I smelled PCP and marijuana in the air. I could see the alcohol bottles being passed around. Finally, Mr. Almighty said, "Take your ass home." He might have thrown in a few explicative words and racially derogatory terms too, but I remember he said, "Take your ass home."

Arthur and Spanky grabbed me and got me out of there so no one could get any parting shots. I was truly thankful those guys stood up for me. In all of my life, I cannot say that I know of any other two people given similar circumstances that stood up for me with such heat in the room, reputations on the line, lines drawn in the sand, and simply an

|9|

intense situation that could have ended horribly. I have seen many men and women that have crumbled and caved in at a fraction of the pressure Arthur and Spanky endured. I learned a great deal about 'code'. The gang stuff has its own code. Arthur and Spanky upheld the code. I was not in their world, I was just a civilian. They did the right thing by speaking up. When I left, I walked through the traditional entrance of the park. When I got to the corner stoplight about a block away, for the first time in my life, I lost consciousness. I was in a kneeling position and someone helped me get up from the sidewalk and asked if I was alright. I was trembling from the shock of this near-death experience. In seconds, I went from being unconscious to full of nervous energy, shaking to get away. I didn't know how to harness the energy, I just ran all the way home and remained shaken the rest of the afternoon.

The end result of that day, and that specific experience, helped shape who I am, my thinking and my life. To me, it was really simple. I don't have to fear any man, any situation, any circumstance, or anything anymore in my life. As terrifying as it was, that day was also the most empowering day of my life. I know I should have got, at minimum, an ass-whooping. They probably would not have shot me, but they would have beaten me to death or inflicted extreme bodily harm. People in our neighborhood, every now and then, would hear of somebody getting beaten to death, afflicted with head trauma, or left permanently paralyzed. For me to live to tell this story without one scratch, I knew from this point on I never had to experience fear after that day in the park. It was my vaccine.

Since that encounter, I have been at gunpoint seven times, caught in between gunfire, attacked with an ice pick and those instances pale in comparison to what I experienced that day. I respect the capability of a weapon. I respect the capability of a group of people. I respect the biggest, most powerful gang: the police. All of those things represent danger and I pay keen attention to them, but fear is created in the mind and I do not subscribe to it.

How to Reason with Fear

At an early age, I began to have a great relationship with fear. Fear and I were honest with each other. I knew when I really was in danger and when I was trippin' and letting fear creep in. Over the years, the chances of fear creeping in have become less and less. Early on, this was not the case. This mental dance with danger and fear was continuous as I navigated South Central Los Angeles. I became fluent in dealing with dysfunction because day in and day out, 24/7, 365 days a year, it was always game on. For instance, I was once chased to class at gunpoint. I know it sounds stupid, but two youngsters actually pulled a gun out on me, I ran and they chased me. Of course, they could have just shot me but I knew they did not want to because they just wanted money. I was scared for sure, but it made me take action, which is what I came to do whenever I was scared. Good, bad, right or wrong, diving into action tends to be my first response. Oddly enough, I was not scared of those two youngsters as they were wannabe gangsters. I was more afraid of how they would get to me after class.

I remember I had a test that day. When I arrived to class, I knew I had to get out of there fast once the class ended. These guys did not want revenge. They were just young kids trying to prove they were tough, which is even more dangerous than if they wanted material things. My only safety would be bolting home the first opportunity I got. The teacher began to distribute the test and said students could leave after they completed their tests. I jetted out of class 20 minutes early to avoid whatever was going to happen when those youngsters came back around. This was the first academic test that I took where I didn't give a second thought to the questions or answers. I never was the type to have test anxiety, but this time was an exception. My anxiety and energy centered around getting out of there, my test score was secondary. I finished in record time. The teacher questioned me a bit but allowed me to leave. I sprinted to the chain link fence that lined the school, climbed it and sprinted half way home to safety. Nothing further happened with those two youngsters. When I received my test score, I was surprised and shocked. I missed the first question and answered the remaining 24 correctly for a score of 96%. I didn't prescribe to thinking I was lucky but I cannot help but think that luck was on my side. This moment built another superpower in me about performing well under pressure. The chase, the gun play and the energy changed my ability to focus, perform, face danger and still strive for excellence. It fueled my power to harness the heightened circumstantial energy and push through any and all scenarios to win. In all my years of being in an educational or professional environment, I cannot say there has been another pressure packed test taking session I would ever experience again. No other tests bothered me after this moment.

Soon after this incident, when I was 13 or 14, another instance of fear versus danger occurred during a 211, armed robbery, at a local burger joint. All of a sudden, a man pulls out a gun and tells everybody to freeze and get on the floor. Me and two of my homeboys, Geno and Steve, were huddled up around the arcade game. Geno was about to take down a high score and was on his last man. As a teenager, he had a big decision to make: take down a high score or take a bullet. For us, it was simple: take down the high score! Steve and I stood between the gunman and Geno so he could finish what he started, and that he did. Geno got his name in the top spot.

It is the little things that make life meaningful even with a dude waving a gun. He did not want to shoot us. He wanted money, but he did not want our money. He went on about his business of robbing the burger joint and Geno went about his business of taking down the high score. Was this dangerous? Yes. Was this something to fear? Not at all. Even in the face of danger, I learned the most important thing to do is to think, not to overreact. Gunplay, robberies, shake downs, punkin' for sport, and potential beat downs were all part of the crazy game of South Central. As all of us got older, we simply had to make a decision about what type of people we would be. By the time I was 13 to 14 years old, I was just willing to die or take an ass-whoopin'. Whether it is a random guy committing a 211 or someone trying to intimidate me, I carried this mentality literally and figuratively through elementary, junior high and high school. I was not the toughest, biggest, or strongest kid and I did not look for trouble. I actually avoided it, but if there was a "fear obstacle" as author Ryan Holiday would say, I made that the way.

I thought the fear obstacles would end when I left South Central and went to Berkeley, CA. They did not. Instead, they just changed forms. The fear obstacles this time were not gangbangers, per se, but the system and its power players—the real gangsters. The University of California, Berkeley was not a good place for me because of the systemic 'isms' and privilege in play. Once again, it was just part of the game, a different game. This was the same during my time later on at the University of Michigan, but it was not as prevalent. My MBA program was for adults, not teens trying to find their way and feeling lucky to even be on the Cal campus and influenced by the culture and people in power.

Oddly enough, I thought that the 'fear factor' tactics were over until I ran into a 'gangster' at my first job out of business school at Chevron. An executive that was at the top of my food chain was just a bully of a guy. The vast majority of people in my workplace were literally scared of him. I had no fear of this dude as I knew he could not kill me, maybe my career at Chevron, but not my life. I actually enjoyed this guy in terms of entertainment. He reminded me of gangbangers in my neighborhood shakin' down scared people just for fun. As part of my development, this executive and I would go to lunch from time to time. His 'come from' was aggressive. He liked to challenge you, trip you up, and go in hard for the mental and intellectual kill. I loved the challenge when I was in his presence. One Friday afternoon, he came back to the office a bit tipsy and called a meeting. The meeting was not really about anything critical, especially for a Friday afternoon with happy hour waiting for me in a couple of hours. I knew tipsy behavioral tendencies, my dad would get tipsy or drunk and talk about nothing just to come down off the high. No big deal. Everyone knows this dude is tipsy so we are just waiting for the meeting to be over. He was going in hard on one woman over nothing and I chuckled. Then he says, "What is so fucking funny Haley?" The look on everyone's face was as if this dude had a gun cocked against my temple. He just didn't know it takes more than words to move me or strike fear in me, which everyone in the room knew he was trying to do. I rose up straight in my chair, looked him in the eye matter of factly and conveyed that we would get everything he wanted done on his desk by Monday. His response was, "Well, all right then." A few minutes after the meeting, the lead in my group, Tom, chewed me up a bit but he coached me on how to complete the assignment over the weekend. Consequently, I worked with the young woman who was chastised to complete the task and made sure it was on his desk on Monday. I never received feedback on that assignment and continued to have a good relationship with the executive—partly because the assignment was not significant, but more so because he could not intimidate me.

I am not going to front, other than South Central, there are three places where my danger radar is super high: Chicago, São Paulo and Rio de Janeiro. My head is on a swivel at all times, eyes focused on everything moving. That's the type of environment everywhere, every second in those cities. Plus, I am a visitor and do not know the terrain like I know Los Angeles, not because I am the target, per se. It is just part of the game in those cities. Those types of environments and my Chevron experience showed me certain people want you to live in fear. It is a power dynamic. I realized this dynamic is built into systemic environments such as Corporate America, governments and places with an established hierarchy.

Fear is a control tool and people want to be able to use it to their advantage. They simply want you to be afraid, which can convey vulnerability mentally, emotionally and physically. Most of us have to work within a system, and I am no different. The people that control the system want dominance in some form or at least want eminent domain over you when they need to evoke power. I will admit that my relationship with fear, not letting it control me, has served me well. But working within systems, I can honestly say that this ability I have has hurt me a few times. Why? People think that because I do not show fear, then that must mean I do not know consequences, repercussions and other concepts that lead to loss, failure, shortcomings, underperformance and the like. This is far from the truth. Coming from a gang-ridden community where your life can be taken in an instant, afforded me a superior understanding of consequences and repercussions. Every now and then, I have come across people that try to use fear as a competitive advantage. I don't fare well with those types. They tend to analyze me for something that simply is not there which makes their own position, life or presence somewhat empty and void of purpose and valor. I know in my mind that I probably should relent.

People, especially in predominantly white institutions, want to be controlling. They want you to think and act as they do. It simply makes the situation comfortable for the system to prevail. This is often tough for me. I cannot help myself or control how other people feel. I revert to speaking my mind, talking up and pointing out what others are afraid to say. I say what others think and I can live with "opportunities" slipping through the cracks because I am more aligned with speaking the truth versus creating comfort for those in power.

Key Takeaways

- Don't let fear rule you. Fear is a natural feeling but do not dwell on it. Face it. Conquer it. By doing so, you make better decisions.

- Focus on *why* uncomfortable situations and people vex you and learn the source of the negativity you're feeling. Oftentimes, it is not the person or situation, it is a predisposition that you must evolve from.

- Do not let others use fear as a way to control you. It is a simple dynamic that many people utilize because it is easy to instill fear in others. When you get comfortable with yourself and your decisions, eliminate fear from their arsenal against you.

3

Rosa was on to Something

> *Do not try and bend the spoon. That's impossible. Instead, only try to realize the truth. There is no spoon. Then you will see it is not the spoon that bends. It is only yourself.*
>
> YOUNG MONK, THE MATRIX

My school busing experience changed my life and shaped my path. I attended my neighborhood elementary school from kindergarten to second grade. From third to sixth grade, I was bused to a predominantly white school in a predominantly white neighborhood. I thought it was a totally different world. Oddly enough, the school was only about a fifteen-minute ride from my house but it might as well have been a 15-hour drive provided the change in environment, culture, tone and manner. The most important difference to me was how I was treated. This was in the mid-70s. The country was a few years removed from the Civil Rights Movement and also the Watts Riots. New communities were being built in newly funded white neighborhoods and along with the rest of the infrastructure, schools were being built as well. Combined with a new federal government push for equality and a need for more students, this meant more government funding. Inner city youth were utilized to fill seats to enable school districts to capture this funding; a great plan when you think of a mechanism to keep schools running proficiently, keeping white female teachers employed, and advancing school district administrators. These were all good things for the system, but the people, communities and families bear the brunt of trying to make clashing philosophies and those 'isms' work harmoniously. It just does not happen, at least for centuries. Take the 13th, 14th and 15th Amendments in 1865 and the 'make good' of the Civil Rights Bills in the late 1960s, things take time. In an effort to provide me a better education, my moms and pops decided to bus me and placed me smack dab in the middle of some funky stuff on the west side of town.

Understanding Power Struggles on an Elementary Level

As I started my educational journey to this distant place, I felt like I had one friend, well actually two. Perry, who was my age and grade, and his sister LaShawn who was one year behind us. There were a few others from the neighborhood who joined us at the bus stop but I did not know them well. When we arrived at our new school, I realized there were about 4 to 5 other buses full of Black students from different parts of LA. My only reference point was what gang set they lived in to determine their geography. In this new place, I had to quickly figure out the other Black folks as well as this new obstacle called white folks. I was inexperienced and uncultured but it did not take me a long time to figure out that the community, students and teachers were not feeling me. I don't want to say they did not like me, but I did feel unwelcome throughout my time at this school. It was not hard-core blatant racism, but there was bad treatment for some and preferential treatment and privilege for others. The one similarity this school had to my neighborhood school and in the streets was 'boys being boys'. I had tons of fights at this school with some of the white boys. The fights were about turf, rule, leadership, straight up punkin' and supremacy. It also was about who was the baddest, Black or white. I will admit, I liked and accepted the challenge. Most of the other Black boys who were bused did not relish in the power struggle. The Black girls did not participate at all or they had their own struggles I was unaware of. In addition to myself, there were only two other Black boys that had zero tolerance for the second class citizenship that the white students, teachers and administrators were trying to dole out to us. Shout out to those boys, now men! It felt good knowing I had back up. Similar to the gangbangers in my hood, the white boys would try to jump you, too! Same tactics, strategies and get down. Essentially, they would try to catch you slippin'. I had my wins and losses. In the end, I gained respect, backed people off me and let everyone know I was not an 'easy out' and you would have to bring it if you came my way.

Of all the years at this school, I would say that my worst year was fourth grade. It seemed like I was in trouble for something every day. It felt like I was in an argument or fight every day. I was in conflict with someone or something. Essentially, I like or love all of my teachers except one, my fourth grade teacher, Mrs. Beard. I don't have fond memories of her at all. It may have been her style, her energy or we simply did not get along, period. It could have been all me creating the friction, I would not put it past my younger self. I recall a time when an aggressive white girl tore a page out of my workbook. I commenced to put her workbook under my foot and tore it in half. Admittedly, I had self-control issues but she started it. She sparked my blaze and I gave few passes back then. My teacher blew up on me big time. I can see her face now, red as an apple. I can hear her voice, blaming me solely and giving the white girl a pass. I can feel her rage, disgust and anger. She personally escorted me to the principal's office. I recall being torched up there as well, but I was accustomed to the principal always having something to say to me. Actually, the principal was a Black woman. You may think that it would have made my time at that school easier but it did not. I always had the feeling that the principal sided against the Black students because of respectability politics. I later realized through my mother, and other parents at the school, that this was the case. This is a dynamic I would experience throughout my academic and professional career. But in this case, I guess I was the type of kid that brought out the worst in educators. Over the years, every now and then, my mother would talk about my fourth grade teacher. No doubt there were some battles between my mother, the teacher and the principal. My behavior was questionable but my academics were always on point, which probably helped me to not get totally dogged out by the school or punished by my parents. Fourth grade was probably the toughest year of my life. It was at that point I realized that authority figures and so-called leaders and helpers in my life may not truly care about my advancement or well-being and could even be detrimental to me.

After fourth grade with my worst teacher, I ended up being in a class with the teacher that saved my life and turned me around. Her name was Mrs. Thrash. She was the only Black teacher at the school and she handled her business in a way that spoke volumes to me. She did not play or let things slide. She demanded the best out of me and my classmates. I was in my third year at the school so I had settled in a bit. Things were moving in slow motion and I was moving at light speed. That year, I had a growth spurt in maturity which had everything to do with being led by a teacher that loved me and wanted me to excel. I do not recall any fighting, issues or principal visits that year. Mrs. Thrash rescued me. God bless her soul. Mrs. Thrash truly created an environment for me to express myself free of risk, to push my boundaries of learning and to discover that I can be in partnership with a teacher and someone crafting my future. It felt like I was unstoppable with Mrs. Thrash on my side.

Everything was great in fifth grade until the end of the year. I recall two events that happened and snapped me back into the reality of where I was physically. The first event was a school 'Mini Olympics' competition. The competition was broken up by grade level and gender. The premier competition was the obstacle course. There are a couple of backstories here. One, the 'All American' during this time was Bruce Jenner. Yes, the former stepdad of the Kardashians, now Caitlyn Jenner. I can recall the marketing push around making Bruce Jenner bigger than life and being the best all-around athlete ever and far more superior than the football, basketball and baseball stars of the era. Second, the aftermath of the television mini-series *Roots* written by Alex Haley. I received my fair share of 'Kunta Kinte' jokes but I was not heavily impacted by it. Mrs. Thrash coached me on dealing with that unique issue I faced by name association. She was an angel in my life. I can't imagine how that year would have ended up without her in my ear. With all that momentum mounting, I was up against the most athletic white boy in my grade. His name was Mike. And honestly, he was a good fighter as we battled for many years exchanging blows. When the gun sounded for the obstacle course, we were pretty much neck and neck the whole way. At the end of the race, there was a 90 degree corner that we could not breach. We both cut the corner and violated the breach but I pulled away from him down the stretch to seemingly be the winner. I will let you imagine which students were pulling for him and which for me. I loved the feeling of crossing the finish line until the administration awarded the white boy the win. It turns out, I automatically disqualified myself when I cut the corner regardless of what he did afterward. I was crushed. Of course, the administration was doing all of this on the fly and modifying the rules to fit their needs and desired outcome. Just part of the game and part of the privilege.

The second event that occurred was when I ran for student body president heading into my sixth grade year. Back then, I had aspirations of leadership within the system. I lost the election but I cannot help but wonder which came first, the chicken or the egg. I had never experienced so much hate, outward dislike and disgust among my own peer group than when I ran for president of that school. In my fifth grade year, I was somewhat of a model student. I knew my fifth grade teacher was not playing around with me in terms of behavior, foolishness, fighting and all the stuff I had done in years past. Plus, I simply didn't want to let her down. When I was running for president, I caught the wrath of boys and girls, both Black and white. By that time, kids had formed crews and some of the Black/white stuff had subsided. We were kids. If you liked someone, it did not matter if they were Black or white once you got to know them. There were a few white kids that I liked just as much as the other Black kids and vice versa. However, the wrath I felt seemed to be an overwhelming response not to the possibility of me winning, but rather me even running. I don't know if I was the first Black person to run for office at that school, and I don't know if another Black person had held an office during my time at the school. One thing for sure, there was a venomous attack around my push for the presidency. When the election results were announced, I took the 'L' in stride. I liked the dude who eventually won. I would call him a school friend because we did not spend time together before or after school or on the weekends. Oddly, I was good with the whole situation until my final semester of high school six years later.

During high school, I had a chance to meet up with a group of other Black teens that attended my old elementary school. It was kind of like a 'what's next for you' hang out. I had loosely kept in contact with some of the students but my guy Perry kept me looped in. We were having a great time and then guess who showed up? Mrs. Thrash! I had lost contact with her so it was phenomenal to see her. She spent time with the group, and then she and I had some one-on-one time to talk. She went on to share the 'real deal' about the elementary school and her struggles as the only Black teacher, dealing with the administration and providing equity to the Black students. Then she dropped a bomb on me. She gave me the gory details of the pressure she was under to not grant me a 'satisfactory' in work habits and cooperation passing grades so that I could not run for school president. I was like, "Well damn, the game is that deep even at the elementary school level?" Even with pre-teens, that 'ism' is a powerful drug. I never would have thought it ran that deep and could be so evil but sadly, I was not surprised.

Well, back to the sixth grade and my final year at this elementary school. It was a good year. I have fond memories of my teacher, good times with the students and the classroom environment was aight. Springtime rolls around and the Mini Olympics competition is upon us again. Same nemesis, new year. My mission was simple, beat him. The gun sounded and we were off. We were neck and neck most of the way until a free throw had to be made before advancing in the obstacle course. His hoop game was weak that day and that's where my guy lost the race. I blew through the obstacle course and would have been the overall winner. I looked back and saw my competition was far behind. I pulled up about two feet from the finish line. In my mind, I had won so I did not care about actually coming in first. I let some of the other competitors cross the finish line before me as I had my back to the finish line watching him, waiting for my guy to get close. His spirit was broken and I could see he was going through the motions. As I shared, he was 'the guy' amongst his crew. This moment was about all of our conflicts over the last four years. This was about the numerous physical and verbal battles we had together. This was about the bullcrap that happened the year prior. This was about the look of defeat on some people's faces watching the competition and the look of pride on others. Yeah, it was bad sportsmanship, poor taste, no honor and all that. I would not support this behavior today, but back then it meant something.

When Mike got within about 5 feet of me, I took two paces to cross the finish line before him. Right then, all hell broke loose--mostly from the white adults. He himself took this moment in stride and not much was said. Over the years, I grew to respect him. He was a tough and worthy competitor. I remember not being able to participate in the medal ceremony. I also remember a parent/teacher conference the next week. My dad, usually a cool customer, was pissed off after that meeting. He wasn't mad at me, but he was pissed off driving home. I never knew why or what was said during that meeting. My thinking is that my pops knew the whole thing was some bullshit. He was probably thinking that after all the crap we endured as a family with this school he has to listen to issues around a race? A race where a white kid simply lost and got a little embarrassed. And, after the numerous issues the Black parents had with the teachers, administrators, white parents and students, my dad was like 'get the f#$% outta here!' We proceeded to drive home, and at my request we did stop at Burger King, so everything was good... Double Whopper with cheese, large fries and strawberry shake. For the rest of sixth grade, life went on as usual. As fate would have it, for the sixth grade school graduation ceremony, my class performed a mini-play about a bill becoming a law or something like that. Guess who they asked to play the role of president? I initially declined the role but my fifth grade teacher stepped in and told me I was doing it. She made a good choice for me. I ended the year on a high note.

Back in my day, the school system was elementary school from kindergarten to 6th grade, junior high was 7th to 8th grade and high school was 9th to 12th grade, as opposed to now where it is K to 5th grade, 6th to 8th grade and 9th to 12th grade. Upon graduating elementary school, my family had a big decision to make. I could continue to be bused to a 'feeder school' or attend my local junior high school. The hood was treacherous in the late-70s and early-80s, it was a war zone on every block and every corner. Being bused was a small reprieve from the terror zones. My parents decided to bus me to a junior high school that even by today's standards of Los Angeles traffic was *so* far from my house. It really and truly felt like I was heading to another country. I remember Monday through Friday when I caught the bus in the morning it was still dark, and when I was dropped off at my bus stop it was dark. Those walks home were risky, to say the least, as the gangbangers and 'freaks' are worse at night. I grew a bit at that time, and with that predators saw threats and opportunities. The threat was about toughness, rival gangbangers and worthy opponents. The opportunity was about change, as in the change in your pocket.

THE BOOK OF DH

With respect to life in junior high, I experienced more of the same stuff in elementary but on a larger scale. There were white students and teachers as well as more Black kids being bused in. My stint at this new junior high school was short lived. I never considered myself as a trouble maker, even when I was painted out to be one in the past. In this new environment, I never picked fights, lashed out or negatively engaged white kids. I just got older and more desensitized to the racism of the time. I did make an effort not to fly off the handle. I wanted to be less edgy, focus on school and other stuff versus white folks and their issues. It just took more to get me enraged and ready to fight. I was older, less volatile, and I began to recognize real threats versus talk and I grew to know my self worth. However, the racial predatory element in this junior high school seemed to find me. There were one or two classes where the path was riddled with white boys that loved talking excessive trash to Black people. I had been somewhat immune to the talk as it did not affect me at that point in my life.

One day, one of the white boys got a little too close and eventually put his hands on me. I went from '0 to 100' instantly. The fight did not end too well for that kid. I had damaged his eye with one tightly-bound punch. As he clutched his eye and his voice screeched due to the pain, I knew I hurt him. After all, I was bigger and stronger. This was my first punch as a teenager with an intent to harm, and it carried all the pent up anger I had shouldered. My fist was balled tight. I felt my fist on his bone and upon impact his head flung back. I knew it was a powerful blow because he was not able to respond. There was no fight in the other kid. I took the wind out of his sails. After striking him, I did not like the feeling. He was actually not one of the hardcore agitators, he was more of a wannabe. He picked the wrong moment and the wrong Black kid to build up his 'rep' with. Soon after, my mom and dad had a meeting with the administration. After which, my pops shared that the resolution to the situation was that I would not be continuing at the school. He also, in so many words, shared that he didn't have the time or the desire to keep running up to my school every time I had a conflict. He expected more out of me. He did not punish me, but the message was clear. This was the last time my dad had to deal with my conflicts regarding a school. I enrolled at my local junior high to finish the 7th grade. While there, I didn't have any social-political conflicts like my last schools, but all the war zone, gangbangin' and neighborhood terrorism was in play. In a weird way, that was easier than the isms.

When 8th grade rolled around, my parents were still determined to bus me. In my day, there was no open enrollment for schools. If you were outside the busing program protocols and wanted to attend a school outside of your neighborhood, you had to use an alternate or fake address. So, we used the address of a friend that would allow me to attend a school that was actually in the neighborhood of my old elementary school. The bus this time was public transportation versus Los Angeles Unified School District buses. The bus stop from my neighborhood to the actual bus ride to the drop off point at the school was one of the most dangerous places to be. Being associated with a public transportation bus was like a zebra being associated with a river. The predators knew the distinct, consistent and necessary moves that the prey would make. And, the same applied to bus riders. The thinking was if you rode the bus you had money in your pocket or a bus pass, which was transferable if you got jacked for it. Lastly, based on your bus route or the address on your bus pass, if the bus pass is 'acquired' the new cardholder would know where you lived and what set you're from, which could be a death sentence. Every day, I had to travel through Blood gang sets–a rival to my home gang set of Crips. Since I didn't grow up with those Black boys, I was totally exposed everyday, especially on the afternoon ride home. Gangbangers would be at multiple bus stops looking for opportunity. This element was the biggest hurdle.

Luckily, heading into high school, my parents were done with the Damon Haley busing experience. I attended George Washington

High School and my graduating class was the very first to graduate from George Washington Preparatory High School. The problems I had experienced being bused or going out of my local area for a quality education were behind me. I may have been a load but the teachers and administration put their arms around me, they loved me and allowed my pattern of growth. I am forever indebted to these beautiful and caring individuals that helped me get on my own track. Now the war on drugs, gangbangin', terrorism and all that was rising, and gunplay and drive by shootings were in full effect. As I shared, I seemed to be okay with handling those elements of life. My high school year launched me to pursue college. Fortunately, I was able to land a spot at Cal Berkeley after the ups and downs of my K-12 educational journey.

Key Takeaways

- There may come a time when the system will not be a good fit. Nevertheless, you will always be expected to perform. Quickly figure out a strategy to navigate the system and perform at your highest level until you can move on.

- Always find your champion. Align with that one person (or team) who truly believes in you and who will help you get through challenges.

- Believe in yourself. Don't let any person, scenario or negative vibe stop you. Keep pushing, driving and excelling. Be proud. Be resilient. Be a winner.

4

Look to the Left, Look to the Right

Captain America: Dr. Banner, now might be a really good time for you to get angry.

David Banner/The Incredible Hulk: That's my secret Captain. I'm always angry.

THE AVENGERS

Stepping foot on Cal's campus was a miracle of sorts. First, I didn't know anything about Cal prior to my senior year of high school. It was simply not on my radar. At best, the only thing on my radar was being an electrician. I owe my pursuit of college to my homeboy Lonnie. He was all in on college being his life after high school. While Lonnie was in the front of the class articulating all the right answers, I was in the back of the class, slouched down in my seat and sportin' a fresh curl and TI (Todd 1) sweatsuit. When Lonnie took the SAT, I did too. When Lonnie applied to UCLA, I asked my college counselor about the UC System. Fortunately, I was academically competitive. As far as my high school classes, I figured that if I'm in class I might as well get A's. Why let the person next to me out work, out think and out-hustle me for a higher grade?

Even as I competed for the best grades, college was not on the top of my to-do list. I was not convinced by college, I knew it was a good thing but I didn't know anyone that could truly vouch for it. Four years just to get a job *and* you pay for it? I was not sold on it completely. Most people I knew got jobs after high school, and I thought my story would be the same. Also, the subject wasn't discussed in my home and none of my siblings attended college. In all the commotion of senior year, I still remember teachers, counselors and the administration pushing college. One day a Cal recruiter was on campus visiting with students during lunch. I had no intentions of attending, but my college counselor sent a student to come grab me. The Cal recruiter happened to be an impressive Black man. His name was Emmitt Scales. I loved everything he said about Cal, the Bay Area, and his community ties to Oakland, CA. I looked at my counselor and asked her, "Is Berkeley a good school?" She said, "Yes, of course." So, I agreed to apply and I was accepted but I was still so far away from my first day of school.

Out of the Hustle, On to Higher Education

The second hurdle happened in the summer of 1984 when the Olympics came to Los Angeles. I was always a hustler and found ways to make money. During this summer, I had a job through a Los Angeles County government program. I financed card and dice games in my neighborhood. I had a hookup that allowed me to sell slightly altered Olympic hats, shirts and accessories, and I had a gig with my big brother Fatty selling event tickets. I was stacking chips. In a short period of time, I had accumulated more cash than I had ever made or got hustling on the street. At the time, I had already opted out of Cal's summer freshmen acclimation program called Summer Bridge. The program was designed for students of color and athletes to integrate into the system over the summer so that the transition in the fall would not be as new and potentially traumatic. It was supposed to provide one a leg up. I was rolling so well during that summer that I second guessed even attending Cal in the fall.

Near the end of the Olympics, some of my workers and I were selling products in the parking lot of the Great Western Forum. I always recruited a lot of workers to canvas the parking lot since fans were clamoring for Olympic paraphernalia. My car was the central meeting spot as well as the location to 're-up' on merchandise. The night was profitable as usual until there was a commotion nearby. People huddled in that location, and I fought through the crowd to see what was happening. Low and behold, it was one of my competitors on the ground bleeding from a stab wound. He was conscious and shared he had been robbed. That issue shifted my ideas of hustling on the streets of Los Angeles and made me think, "Well, maybe heading to Cal is not a bad idea after all."

After a great summer, it was time for me to start a new adventure called Cal. My dad and I packed the car, I said my goodbyes to family and friends and we headed up north. I remember the long drive of nothingness on Interstate 5 then getting to the city of Berkeley. People seemed pleasant. It had a nice small town feel and environment. The residential housing staff was bubbly, cheery and upbeat. I checked into my dorm room. After which, my dad took me to a nearby grocery store and loaded me up with non-perishable food to stack under my bed and closet in my dorm room. My dad was a pretty pragmatic guy, loving but purpose driven. Once the vitals were handled, he headed back to Los Angeles within a few hours of arriving at the dorm. That was the first time in my life I essentially felt on my own. Hours passed and I soon began to panic. I had not seen one Black person in hours. The white folks were cool and friendly, but I was just uncomfortable with the whole scene of nothing being familiar. Finally, in the distance I saw a Black woman. I sprinted her way and introduced myself. Her name was Bertha Cross. She was from Los Angeles and graduated from Crenshaw High School. She too was a freshman and was well-liked by many. She attended the Summer Bridge program and knew the lay of the land. We lived in the same dormitory and had a fair amount in common. She was my guide and go-to for the next few days.

After a day or two of registration and student administration stuff, the day many aspirants were looking forward to for years was upon us…the first day of college. I felt a myriad of emotions but mostly I was hyped, curious, and nervous. The actual class sizes and number of students were huge! I had never seen so many people seated in one place to learn. I expected a large number of white students but the shocker was I did not expect so many Asian students. They seemed to outnumber the Black students. My naivety had me thinking 'Black and white' but I quickly got over that. I think I had four classes my first semester. In at least two of my classes, and it was a trend at Cal during that time, the professor would say, "Take a good look at the student on your right and at the student on your left. One of them probably will not be here by the end of the semester or at graduation." I always thought that was some bullcrap to say. However, I was unaffected. I had heard more vicious, negative, intimidating stuff in elementary and junior high school. My street knowledge, 'family metal' and the voice I held inside said, "Bring it then." Plus, when I heard challenges, attacks and bullcrap assertions that were directed at me, I have always been motivated by a scene from one of my favorite movies *The Mack*, which is a 70s blaxploitation classic. There is a scene when the star of the movie Goldie, who is a pimp, is talking to his friend, who is played by G.O.A.T comedian Richard Pryor. Goldie says to his friend, "I just can't get it in my head how a woman can walk the street every night, even in the rain, and take a chance on getting robbed or sent to jail or getting her arm broken by a sadistic fool from the suburbs and she gets all that money and takes it to some dude. I just can't figure it out." As a response, his friend says, "Your game is strong, baby."

Then Goldie says, "Well, I ain't talking about me. I'm talking about those other pimps."

Are you saying I am not going to finish the semester or graduate from Cal? Yo professor, you ain't talking about me. You talking about the people to the left and right of me! But hey, game on!

Becoming Invisible to Dodge the Whip

Cal in the mid-80s was not a charming place for the average Black student. There were undertones around affirmative action and the question of credibility of a Black person's acceptance into Cal, even if you were on an athletic scholarship. Simultaneously, there was the emergence of Black culture seeping into mainstream culture. Then, there were guys like me 'crashing the party'… a first generation college student, not knowing my place as a second-class citizen to white people. I came into this arena not understanding how Black people are supposed to act to make white folks comfortable by feeling happy just to be there and going along to get along. There were tons of day-to-day manageable battles with being a party crasher but one day quickly forced me to pivot if I was going to fit in, get along and excel at Cal.

The lecture style classes were huge and impersonal. You seldom had a chance to have access to the professor. Yeah, there were office hours but unless you were there early to stand in line, one would never meet with the professor one-on-one. So, the classes were broken down into sections that were taught by graduate school students. Usually, sections met twice per week. I had taken a midterm test and the test scores would be distributed by the graduate in the next section. The following week, I was late to the session and had to sit on the floor. Side note, the first two years at Cal taught me to be on time. If you were late, finding a seat in a lecture or section was damn near impossible. So, the grad assistant begins to talk about the test, grading and feedback on the overall class response to the test questions. Imagine, this was the first test results at Cal for many of us. The energy of these high performers, perfectionists, wannabes and actual future leaders of the world was palpable as we waited on pins and needles for this person to shut up and give us the test scores. I was half way listening to her while she described exemplary responses to a few of the test questions by one of the students in the room. Then finally I heard her say, "Is Damon Haley here today?" Damn, I was as stunned as all the other students when they realized she was talking about me. The real stunner was when I saw the look on her face when she realized who I was. I got a good look as I stood up from the back of the class and made my way to the front to retrieve my test. By the time I got to her, the wind was out of her sails. She was lifeless, speechless, and dejected. It was almost like she had forgotten what she just said. She merely handed me my test paper. She did not look at me. She commenced to call out names as the other students collected their tests.

The testimony by the graduate assistant turned out to be a curse. After that, I heard snide comments when I was late to a session or when I asked questions...and participation was part of the grade. My two subsequent tests had so much red ink on them I thought she slit her wrist while she was grading my paper. My final grade was not to my liking. She 'pencil whipped' me, which is a term used when the person who is keeping score cheats while scoring one's points. This made me truly feel that Cal and this college thing was some bullcrap. I felt this game was rigged just like it was in elementary school. That if you are Black and a high performer, you better be acceptable or show up in the vision of how the powers that be want you to be. That was cruel and blatant racism toward a teenager who was looking at enduring this system for 3 more years. The realities I faced went against everything Cal supposedly stood for. I was twisted up. From then on, I realized my survival and advancement would depend on being anonymous. My key lesson after that class? Sadly, it was don't ever let the professor know your name or connect your face with your name. The messaging was already out there that professors were trying to weed out students. The other dynamic was which students were going to receive A's and B's? The bell curve of grading was such that most of the students were destined to receive C's. I learned to be on full alert early at Cal; let my work speak for itself and not my physical presence.

What Does 'Culture Fit' Really Mean?

In high school, I read the book *The Invisible Man* by Ralph Ellison. Powerful book! I would sneak to talk to my high school English teacher at lunch and recess to talk about metaphors, similes, analogies and meanings hidden within the text. I felt that at Cal I had to play it like an invisible man while dealing with the 'systems' and 'isms'. I had to focus and reveal my true self on my own time. I was a glutton for system, isms and privilege 'punishment' though.

Heading into my sophomore year, I tried out for the Cal baseball team. I was a pretty good baseball player in high school. I was All League and All City as a senior. My team made it to LA's Final Four, but we failed one game short of playing for the City Championship at Dodger Stadium. A few of my high school teammates were drafted by major league baseball teams and a few played college locally. As for me, I was getting a good look from the Cincinnati Reds but did not get drafted. The only college I recall that was interested in me was Arizona State, but I did not reciprocate the interest. I was inspired to try out for Cal's team by one of my neighborhood friends. His brother, long time MLB player Claudell Washington, encouraged me as well. Plus, MLB stars like Eric Davis, Darryl Strawberry, Chili Davis and Eddie Murray were all from South Central LA and promoted baseball to young aspiring players. So, that summer in between hustling for money I also worked out, practiced at the park and was a regular at the batting cage. When fall semester began, I was ready. As with most tryouts for walk-ons, there are tons of hopefuls. Everybody trying out was pretty good in high school...not to mention the incumbents returning for the upcoming season. I matched up pretty well with the other players in terms of my skills, athletic abilities, hitting, catching, etc. My biggest challenge was culture fit.

In high school, we talked and expressed ourselves throughout practice and games so I thought it was normal. It was not. I will admit I was very 'hood', used colorful words to cope with nervousness and discomfort. More importantly, I did not know this 'robotic' baseball culture that seemed to be in play at Cal. A few of the other Black players trying out respected me and my game but thought I was funny. It was almost like they were laughing at me and not with me. The white players looked at me perplexed and did not engage me. It was not until I made the winter squad team that I was pulled to the side by a white player who had been with the team previously and also lived in my dorm. We both were outfielders so we spent a lot of time together at practice. In essence, he broke me down from my joking and chattering on the field, to the unwritten dress code at practice. I never knew that I could not cut my stirrups and wear them thin up to my knee. I was basically all 'backwards' other than my actual performance on the field. I was grateful to this teammate and friend taking the time to set me straight as I was oblivious to all the game he put me up on with respect to Cal's brand of baseball, the head coach, our position coach and the returning Cal players.

My time on Cal's team was short lived. The coach never articulated the 'look to your left, look to your right' credo but it was in full effect. Most of the players I started the journey with on day one seemed to drift each week. I tried to fit in but I simply did a poor job at doing so. I was on the team, but it did not feel like I was part of the team. My 'white confidant' was truly dialed in. He shared why I was moved from one outfield position to the other and how our position coach acquiesced to the players' demands to get reps and opportunities versus working with a new, young player. At the time, there were five Black players on the team, me and another Black guy were outfielders. My friend would always say that I should act like the other Black guy. He was quick to share how I should act in relation to the other Black guy but never once did he convey how the white coaches and our teammates should simply act fairly. He never mentioned how the coaches and team could have treated me like one's player, one's teammate and actually personify the 'team talk' that was spoken during practice, before games and during team activities. Admittedly, the other Black guy was simply being himself and we were just different individuals. He was happy, jovial and seemed to integrate with the system better than me. I do not think that the culture fit was a stretch for him as his 'come from' with the other players was more aligned than mine. And, I was not mad or offended by my friends' comments at the time. I was totally open to the feedback and he was 'spitting game' I desperately needed. I would admit that at 19, I was a bit 'unseasoned' at code-switching and the social skills necessary to thrive in a predominately white system. And on the flip side, many of the coaches and teammates were uninterested in understanding, relating or getting to know the real me. With all of that said, the Cal system, isms and 'privilege' was still at work...and possibly working overtime.

During an inter squad game, I hit a frozen rope off the wall and slid into third base for a triple. I was a bit 'spirited' after the hit. Spirited, not disrespectful, per se. I took a lead off third base and the pitcher tossed the ball to the third baseman. The third baseman caught the ball and tagged me hard right in the face. To put it lightly, I took exception to it. I was not expecting it. I gave him a little something he did not expect. I was immediately benched after our exchange and that was followed up with a meeting with my position coach. I was unaware that the 'glove punch' was proper protocol when a player hits a triple or double and that I should have protected myself. I would expect that bullcrap move from a competitor, but not from a teammate. My response to the coach was to the effect of, "Cool. He should have protected himself too." In short, it did not create a good look for me. The third baseman was the star of the team, the coach was siding with him and I looked like the bad guy in front of the entire team. Essentially, it was the beginning of the end for me with the team. Needless to say, my number of reps of practice seemed to decrease along with my playing time in inter squad and other winter games. There was some questionable coaching that occurred for about two weeks. At the time, I chalked it up as part of the game. As for me, I became unnecessarily belligerent and was not handling the situation well at all. I always think to myself "they got me" whenever I think of this experience. The Cal Baseball Team had broken me. I was not doing well on the field or in the classroom. I initiated another one on-one with my position coach. My impression of my position coach was that he was cool and crafty with his words and played things neutral and was not down for me. He knew the right things to say to deflect my real issues, be politically correct and protect the program. During our meeting, I made a reference about wasting my time. At the end of the next practice, the head coach shared that there would be another cut to trim the team roster because he did not want to 'waste anyone's time'. Of course, when I checked the roster the next day there were two less members on the team...me and another guy that I learned was academically ineligible. I was not an undeniable, phenomenal talent and probably would not have made it to the MLB. Did I have enough talent to remain on the team that year and through my college years? Maybe, maybe not. As I reflect back on the experience, and it was truly invaluable, I know 'they got' that teenage boy. Cal Baseball threw me off my game and eroded 17 days of my life. Between how things played out, the dance with my position coach and the inside information received from my white teammate, I did not recognize the rules and nuances of the Cal Baseball game. My white friend was the most valuable element of the process, and he truly tried to coach me up to survive the system the best he could. I know he cared about me and his integrity was impeccable. Bless him. When we were Cal Baseball teammates, at some point, he looked to his left and then to his right, and I was gone.

After my Cal Baseball experience, I quickly jumped back on track. Fortunately, there were a couple of people on the Cal campus that helped me tremendously. The first was a well-known Black social scientist that was a subject matter expert on race, academics and sports. He helped me lick my wounds and shared the harsh realities of the challenges that I was facing with Cal Baseball, a non-revenue generating NCAA sport and the history of treatment of Black people in sports. In addition, two other Black men on campus were vital to my healing. They inspired me to embrace my best self and helped to kick-start me into my future. Both were on the educational performance and support staff at Cal. One was a mathematical genius and he singlehandedly increased the numbers of successful Black graduates in engineering, science and technology at Cal. The other amazing support staff member was a savvy business and economics aficionado who enabled many Black students to excel at Cal and beyond. He also employed me for a couple of years while I was at the university. As I rebounded and ventured to declare a major, I was heavily influenced by the aforementioned 'Econ Guy' and thus I decided to pursue Economics as a major. I was a bit skeptical of the Economics Department because I was 'pencil whipped' by being given a lower grade than I earned. The professor owned up to the error but never changed my grade.

Nevertheless, upon learning the requirements for automatic acceptance, I had to obtain an 'A' in two upcoming classes. I dug in like never before. My life was solely about getting an A in these two classes. My roommate at the time was my fraternity and line brother Brian. He was locked in too. Brian was competing to be, and later became, Cal's first modern day Black starting quarterback. As I committed to class and homework, I saw Brian lift weights and build his body. He also was on the field throwing routes and calling plays. Then, at night he reviewed film. Our spot was a football house. I even learned the offensive plays, knew the defensive call-outs Sam, Mike, Whip, etc. It was the best form of television for me back then. I was inspired and motivated seeing this side of football. Learning about what a quarterback does was a good change of pace from my classwork. And, I was 100% in support of Brian winning the starting job and leading Cal Football. So as he went hard, I went harder. In the end, I received two A-grades. In one class, I truly was not perfect. Plus, there were a few other students that were a bit sharper than me. I was resolved with that grade. The other A- I was not comfortable with. I know I crushed the midterms and homework, and I thought I crushed the final exam. I committed my cardinal sin of letting the professor know who I was because I needed to discuss my final exam grade with him. The one question we disputed had to do with the inelasticity and elasticity of a good. I used an example of crack cocaine as an inelastic good in that you can pay a set price for a set amount at the top of the hour, but then the next hour you can pay a higher price for the exact same amount. Now, I never sold crack, hand to God, but I was aware of the marketplace and economics around the business. After sharing, the professor was truly shocked. He simply was unaware of this type of business. He did communicate that I was absolutely correct in my breakdown of the economic principles. Sadly, he was forthright and stern that under no conditions would he give me full credit for the exam response or an A in the class because he could not condone that subject matter as part of his class and instruction. He pencil whipped me, but he looked me in the eye doing it and was honest. I respected him for that. Also, he was true to his word and provided me with a written reference to accompany my Economics application. Overall, he was a good dude. Unfair and rigid in thought, but a good dude. I accomplished my goal of receiving automatic acceptance. I was unaware of the Economics Department policy of rounding up to arrive at a designated GPA in select classes. I was able to not leave my acceptance into the major in the hands of a committee, judges, subjectivity, etc. Life was good for me upon being granted access into the Economics major.

By the time I was an Economics major, I had experienced and figured a lot of things out about myself, life, Cal and its system of isms and privilege. I was not a fan of the academic culture, negativity and bias, but at least it no longer surprised or shocked me like it did earlier in my time there. Even within my major, I still avoided professors to a degree. I kept my head down and just did my work until I had one class where I would go to the professor's office hours and tell him my name was Mike. I would avoid mentioning my last name and would stick to questions and clarifications based on the classwork.

The funny thing is that even though I told him my name was Mike, he still referred to me as the other Black guy in his other class. To clarify, this professor taught the same class twice that semester. He had a Black guy in each of his two classes. Even by white folks 'all brothers look alike standards', we looked nothing alike. One day, I broke discipline. I slipped up. No, I fucked up. The professor called me by the other Black guy's name and I blasted him. He probably did not deserve or warrant what I gave him on that day. There were other students in the office so I literally did put him on blast. Plus, I let him build the reputation of calling me out of my name so I should have checked him before the momentum started. With that said, he didn't only pencil whip me, he stabbed me in the neck with the pencil...twice. I did not get a passing grade that semester and had to retake the class. And to add insult to my grade point injury, the next time I took the class my graduate assistant essentially shared that regardless of what I get on my tests the highest grade I would receive was a C. Even though grading should always be unbiased, I accepted that as I knew I had made a mistake with that professor. True, I gave him the impetus to dog me out but it was still unfair. A grade is a grade and should be applied fairly, not driven by the scrutiny of an office hour disagreement. Impartial grading? Nope! Totally allowed by the system? Yep! This was some bullcrap...again. Once again, all of this mission and vision of Cal being a coveted destination of higher learning was all a disguise of words and actions. Cal was just another system applying isms and privilege to its white professors and students to crap on whoever they felt like. And the graduate assistant? She was just sending the message. She was not the messenger. "Don't hate the player. Hate the game"...that is a street code. It was some bullcrap because she was in on the bullcrap too. She handled it with honor, dignity and reality...in a system, ism, privilege way. She held her word and 'assigned' me a passing grade so it was on to the next thing.

When it was my time to graduate, it truly was a graduation for me. I had, and still have, no love lost for Cal. The systems, isms and privilege did their thing. And, from what I gather, it is still doing its thing. The people I met at Cal were phenomenal and for that, I am grateful. The environment was a big, highly competitive, treacherous, hierarchical jungle where only the strong shall survive. After my last final exam, it felt like a 800 pound gorilla jumped off my back. To blow off some steam and celebrate, I joined one of my frat brothers at a local bar. Like many other students celebrating, we were drunk, loud, boisterous and acting like 20 year olds. We decided to do some bar hopping. My celebration was cut short by the Berkeley Police. I thought that 'gangbangin' was behind me. I thought I had seen the last gun in my face back in my neighborhood, but I was wrong. The police actually plucked me out of the rowdy crowd when a warning would have sufficed. Not only did they harass me, but to actually draw a firearm out on a student at Cal during finals week was insane. I was *so* done with Cal. When I walked across the graduation stage at Cal, I felt I owed Cal nothing. Other than a copy of my degree, it owed me nothing. We were even. As I reflect back with sadness, I saw a fair amount of students to the right and left of me not finish with me. I even knew two people that took their own lives on Cal's campus. Shame on those professors who said that look to your right and look to your left bullcrap! That's not the way to catapult students to excellence. But hey, like Goldie says, they were not talking about me, they were talking about those other students.

Key Takeaways

- Always believe and bet on yourself. Don't compromise who you are and what you stand for. You have been built up and crafted to be who you are with the life experience you have gained. Don't start over for anyone or anything, unless *you* want to improve yourself.

- Remember that it is not quitting if you 'get out' while you are ahead. Sometimes, you have to jump before the end of the ride. Sometimes the driver(s) will not take you where you need to go.

- When you know you are in someone's game, do not get emotional. Learn the rules, understand how to win, game plan, and execute the win.

5

Wrong Time. Wrong Situation. Wrong Guy.

> *Never let success go to your head. Never let failure get to your heart.*
>
> — BEYONCE KNOWLES-CARTER

Upon graduating from Cal, like most students, I was in pursuit of not just full-time employment but a unique opportunity that carried a tremendous upside with a great company. Fortunately, my Economics major allowed me to compete with other students in Cal's business school for premium job interviews with the nation's most notable companies. San Francisco was just across the Bay and was a west coast home for many multinational business entities. I fared pretty well with landing quality, high potential interviews. I also did well with the on-campus interviews. Where I fell short was the company on-site interviews, which were mostly in San Francisco and Oakland. I could not really put my finger on what was the issue and why I did not secure more offers. I was a firm believer in working with Cal's Career Planning and Placement Office and took full advantage of the services, staff and resources. As I recall, the office did an excellent job in helping me write my resume and cover letters, mining for good job interview fits and coaching me on the ins and outs of interviewing. I received a few sales job interviews in Oakland upon graduation, but I had my eye on three jobs that seemed to slip through my fingers.

Never Be Defeated: Facing Rejection

The first was an accounting job with Price Waterhouse. I made it to the final round and they opted to hire other candidates. I was short 2 or 3 accounting classes versus an accounting major in the business school, but they knew that when I was selected to be part of the on-campus interview slate and the on-site interview in San Francisco. I still was prepared. Mentally, I was ready. I had the blue suit, red tie and white shirt as well as the black socks and shoes. I was confident. The Price Waterhouse interviews and lunch session felt right. There was great energy, eye contact, humor, shop talk and all that. I was disappointed when the young lady that interviewed me on campus, and who was my on-site host, broke the news that other candidates were selected and I wasn't. I cannot recall the specific feedback she provided, maybe because it was my first true job-related rejection and disappointment. I zoned out after she told me the bad news. Nothing else she said was strong enough to resonate with me. One thing was certain, I was the wrong guy for the job.

The second instance of defeat occurred during my quest to secure employment with Arthur Andersen, which is now Accenture. Once again, I crushed the on-campus interview and had been invited to the San Francisco office. Then, the invitation came in the midst of one of my visits back to Los Angeles. I shared this with the recruiter and since they needed to interview me quickly, they offered to fly me from Los Angeles to San Francisco for the day. This was totally new terrain for me. I truly felt honored to receive this type of interest. I felt really good about the interview and I was a happy dude at the end of the day. When I returned to the Bay Area, I received word from the recruiter that a high-ranking executive at Arthur Andersen wanted to interview me. My anticipation was heightened even more, I couldn't help but think they were highly interested in me. My concern was that I only had one suit and one white shirt, and that I would be wearing the same outfit three times for interviews with one company. I met with the executive and a few members from his team. The style of interview was a case method. Most of the questions were client-related scenarios and 'what if' scenarios. After the interview, I was feeling good but not great. I didn't think I nailed it but I still thought I did pretty well. I was accustomed to only being rewarded with exceptional performances so my hopes of securing the job was 50/50. When I received the 'guillotine call' from the recruiter, my gut was right. Arthur Andersen selected other candidates ahead of me. In this case, I was prepared to probe the recruiter for feedback. The recruiter explained my case succinctly and eloquently. He thanked me for my patience for interviewing three times and my preparedness for each interview, as well as hopping on a flight for the second interview. He shared that I was a great candidate, and that I should be proud of making it to the final round of interviewing since Arthur Andersen's selection process was the most rigorous in the industry. And then reality hit, the recruiter shared that other candidates simply did a better job with the executives and their case method responses. I did not rank high enough to be extended an offer after that point. The recruiter explained the 'boogie prize' that if someone had declined their offer, I would have an opportunity to revisit employment with Arthur Andersen. Once again, I was the wrong guy.

The third and most coveted opportunity that did not work out for me was with the investment bank, Houlihan Lokey. It was my long shot. I honestly felt my resume at the time was weak because I had not had 'big time' summer internships heading into my request to be placed on the on-campus interview schedule. Candidates were required to submit a one-page essay along with an official transcript. The protocol for learning if you had been accepted to interview on-campus was similar to when I tried out for the Cal baseball team. The business school posted the interview schedule outside its office. If your name was on the schedule, you were awarded an interview. Boom! My name was on the list. Leading up to and during the interview, I gave it everything I had. The day of the interview, I recall a former Cal graduate was on-campus as part of Houlihan Lokey's interviewing team. I did not know him well, but we had a class or two together and we recognized one another. I felt even better about my chances. Again, the interview felt good. I thought the interviewer was sharp, I asked great questions, was cordial and had personality. After the interview, I was told to circle back to check the list on the wall for those candidates that would be continuing with the interview process. The list would contain the names of candidates who would be invited to dinner that night at a local restaurant blocks from Cal's campus. I was on pins and needles that day wondering if my name would be posted. Boom! I was heading to dinner with Houlihan Lokey!

When I arrived at dinner, everything was perfect. It was an upscale restaurant that I had only passed by before and always wondered about the dining experience. There was a private room, everyone was nice and bubbly...it was an intimate affair. Then, I saw someone I could not believe was in the room. It was a white guy that lived in the dorm with me when I was a sophomore. We were in the same Intro to Economics class and he bombed the first midterm and dropped the class. I knew because we studied together. He majored in Political Science or History...not a Business, Economics or a quantitative major like most of the interview candidates. I totally did not understand. My mind could not connect the dots. The room was full of candidates trying to prove their intellect to be worthy of a job in investment banking, the most coveted gig coming out of Cal.

Flash forward a few weeks. I got the nod for the on-site interview, but I did not get the job offer. My feedback on my shortcomings was pretty light. I can recall the recruiter sharing that they leaned towards engineers and mathematics majors in the final selection process. I was down but not out. I just figured I did not amplify my quantitative skills with respect to econometrics, accounting, finance, etc. I competed well and knew I had to be near perfect, and I was not. Flash forward a few more weeks, I see Mr. Political Science/History major. We talk for a bit and then I ask him about his Houlihan Lokey experience. He shared he got the job! I congratulated him but got the hell out of there quick, fast and in a hurry. I was hot and fuming! First off, I could not believe this guy made it onto the interview schedule, let alone getting the job offer. Then, I thought about all that bullcrap the business school representatives were sharing about Houlihan Lokey and how they only hired the best. And, all that mess the recruiter shared about the final decision making criteria and leaning towards engineers and the like. It was all propaganda. I consulted with my Career Planning and Placement 'insider' to give me more perspective on the recent hirings, which required some shopping around the business school. I learned that Houlihan Lokey did indeed extend offers that did not align with the type of students the recruiter originally targeted. It was the old 'move the target trick'. I also learned that systems, isms and privilege was in play once again because there were also no Asian students on the interview schedule despite numerous submissions. Very odd given that I know my Asian colleagues were beasts in all of my economics and business classes. The rules changed for some and I was part of the some. I was a 'big boy' about the situation and eventually cooled off. And of course, I became the wrong guy again in the wrong situation.

Finding the Right Fit Takes Time

After the 'round robin' interview process at Cal, I landed two job offers, and I gave only one serious consideration. Luckily, on a visit to Los Angeles, I bumped into one of my high school counselors, Mrs. Roy. I shared my interviewing and job offer woes and she connected me with one of her friends in education as an opportunity after graduation. I talked to her colleague, David Morgan, who was the Associate Director of Admissions at Occidental College. I immediately fell in love with David, and I'm still in love with him. He shared information about the position of Admissions Officer and that given my interest in sports I could have involvement with the Athletic Department to bolster my experience. Also, I would be traveling frequently to the Southeast part of the U.S. and to Northern and Southern California as part of my job responsibilities. The job would be located in Los Angeles, and I could work from home some days. And there was more. David shared that for the first time in the history of Occidental College, they recently hired a Black president. Education was not my first choice, but this position was exactly what I felt I needed. I projected that David would be a phenomenal mentor and brother, which he was and still is to this day. The traveling aspect seemed 'sexy' to me. Growing up in Los Angeles and going to school in the Bay Area, I did not get around much. I hadn't been out of the state at that point in my life. When I accepted the job, I was in my early 20s and was able to experience traveling to Atlanta, Miami, New Orleans, Charlotte, San Diego and back to the Bay Area, all on the company dime. The pay was not robust but the experience was invaluable. David, and his wife who was Occidental's Financial Aid Director, poured so much into me professionally and personally. Being in the academic environment kept me sharp and well studied. Occidental College was a small school with a tight knit group of people. The entire executive, administrative, athletic and teaching staff were extraordinarily remarkable. The President, John Slaughter also took a liking to me. Our exchanges and his role modeling lit my fire. Also, being in Los Angeles and plugging back into family and friends helped restore my soul after my grueling, draining Cal experience. I was only at Occidental College and in Los Angeles for one year. I was accepted to the MBA Program at the University of Michigan at Ann Arbor. Sure as the sun was rising in the east, Occidental College came at the right time and I was the right guy! This is how life works sometimes, you get unexpected opportunities that end up being the perfect fit.

Coming off my Occidental College and Los Angeles experience, I was totally ready to take on Michigan's MBA program. I had never visited Ann Arbor but everyone, not 99.9%, but everyone as in 100% had glowing, passionate high regards for the University of Michigan. I talked to an array of undergraduate, law and business school representatives and graduates, and they all were stoked on Michigan. I had been accepted to the University of Texas at Austin MBA program, waitlisted at Stanford, and was negotiating with USC. My Econ Guy at Cal was pushing Harvard to me hard as he had shepherded a few Black guys there from Cal. Talking to people about these other schools paled in comparison to the energy, support and shear rave about Michigan. I was set to be a Wolverine. In the first week; it did not disappoint. I was matched up with a 'buddy' through the Black Business Students Association (BBSA). My buddy was James, who was a second year MBA student and the BBSA president. Upon our introduction, James asked me, "Why did you come to Michigan?" I gave him the spiel about higher education and learning more about business. James was like, "Naw, bruh. You came here to get a job and get paid." My response, "Yeah, you're right." From that point on, that goal became my focal point. I needed to learn so that I could compete. I needed to perform well so I could 'match up' with my business school comrades when the time came to get a summer internship and a full-time job. However, getting the job was about the nuances that I missed, did not acquire and did not recognize at Cal. During my time in Michigan, it had the largest Black MBA enrollment of the top five business schools in the country. We were deep and diverse in terms of intellect, talent, experience and all the vital elements to make our community within the business school strong and powerful. Not to discard, reject, negate or demean the Michigan MBA system, white students or any other student groups, but at the highest levels of competition, opportunity and money making, there needs to be that element of 'insider trading' in the form of information, best practices, relationships, training and education that provides the edge. The strength in the numbers of Black students in the Michigan MBA program provided the edge that white students for centuries, routinely enjoyed at Michigan.

I was one of the youngest men in the MBA program. I had great big sisters and brothers in the program who loved me, schooled me, were patient with me and helped me mature quickly. I fell in line accordingly. I remember my good friend Val, she reviewed my resume and cover letter during the first few weeks at Michigan. Val was tough, sharp, smart, quick and didn't hold back anything from anybody. She was from Chicago and did not play. Val balled up both my resume and cover letter and threw it at a trash can, she missed and I rebounded it. Val gave me more insight in 40 minutes than I had received in four months working with Cal's Career Planning Center. Together, we worked to create an exceptional expression of my value to a company. Early on at Michigan, it was a turning point of how I viewed the educational and job search process. It was all love. Val still shoots me business ideas to grow my businesses. My guy Don essentially told me what to do, what to say and how to do it. He was more 'seasoned' than most students and had been where I was going in terms of manhood, professional development and lifestyle. I listened and learned, period. Don is still my guy. These classmates were second year MBAs but my first year MBA peers were just as impressive and impactful. Leading the way was my roomie, my homeboy, Ron. He was a magnificent brother, student, professional, thinker and leader. He had an exceptional ability to enter into any conversation with worthwhile thought and proper perspective regardless of whether he was speaking with administrators, students, recruiters, the maintenance crew or the guy on the local corner. I soaked it all in and still do to this day. There are too many other great women and men that helped shape me from my Michigan days, bless all of them. The Occidental College and Michigan experience provided me with an amazing turnaround from my Cal days. And more importantly, I figured out the language, tendencies, habits, reading between the lines, and hidden verbal and nonverbal messaging and messages of the systems, isms and privilege as it pertained to Corporate America, professional white folks and the code switching Black people had to perfect to effectively compete for premium opportunities upon graduating from Michigan. As a result of my receiving a cultivating and 'true education' at Michigan, I was able to secure the job of my choice at Chevron Corporation's Global Headquarters. On top of that, I was heading back to the Bay Area. It was the right time, it was the right situation and, of course, I was the right guy!

The only blemish on an otherwise fantastic experience at Michigan was the civil unrest associated with the verdict of the Rodney King trial in the early 90s, which occurred days before graduation. Similar to me finishing my last class at Cal, the Rodney King verdict deflated my academic accomplishment. It was a somber time in our country and in the Black community. We all saw the video of King being beaten by police. I stood before my fellow Black classmates on the morning of our graduation and a day after the Rodney King verdict. The president of the Black Business Students Association, Ron Chandler, appointed me to address the organization hours before our official school graduation. I had my notes ready to address this impressive group of women and men who had given their heart and souls to earn their master degrees. As I began my speech, I was overwhelmed by the LA Riots and a sea of emotions captured the moment. I was far from home and about to be awarded a great educational honor but I couldn't help but to think about my people, my community and all of the issues around the Rodney King beating and verdict. Of course, I went off script and began to encourage my classmates to make a difference in our world and community in addition to following their personal pursuit of career, financial gain and the rights and privileges of an MBA from Michigan. I definitely provided a spirited rally cry for my fellow classmates. To this day, I am still reminded by many of my friends of this speech.

We, the new leaders and an accomplished group of soon to be business executives at a high point in our lives, had to grapple with riots occurring in nearby Detroit and every major metropolitan area in the USA. But, I remained optimistic about my journey at Chevron and in the Bay Area. In between my first and second year at Michigan, I secured a summer internship at Chevron. The internship was a quasi-audition for a full-time offer with Chevron after graduation. I was afforded a great internship experience and it would have taken an off the charts full-time offer from another company to shift my thinking away from Chevron. My internship was with the Competitor Analysis group. I would meet with my manager every Monday for marching orders and we would circle back on progress midday on Thursdays. In terms of my overall summer assignment, I had to construct a competitor analysis and ranking of 4 - 6 oil companies based on prescribed areas of finance, business operations and publicly available future projects. In addition, the internship class would have periodic lunches, seminars and meetings to scale our understanding of Chevron and the oil industry. All of that was fine and dandy, but the highlight of my summer was interacting with four Black Chevron executives who really schooled me in terms of how to win at Chevron and navigate the corporate landscape. First, my main guy was Percy. He actually grew up in my old neighborhood and we both still had ties there so we had the 'homeboy' connection. Percy was saucy and had that low key LA bravado that I loved. Then, there was Greg who was for many years the highest ranking Black executive at Chevron. Greg was a diplomat and a strategist. He knew how to uncover, unlock and resolve any problems. Third, was my guy Bill. He simply had swag and talked like a 70s player in a blaxploitation movie. He was that cool uncle that let you stretch the limits when you were a teenager. Last, but not least was Dollar Bill. We worked in the same proximity during my summer internship. Dollar Bill went to work on me all summer. Everyday he gave me something to grow on in the form of tangible finance and accounting strategies, business operation insights and organizational structure. He was the reason my work was excellent and my final project was exemplary. These four guys were the true reason I felt I could truly excel and win at Chevron despite the system, isms and privileges these elements always seem to pose together.

My primary job entering Chevron full-time was being a member of the Finance Development Program. For the first two years, I would have four 6 month assignments. My first assignment with Chevron was with the Treasury Group. I was led by two great minds and professional men, Jim and Tom. I reported to Jim on a day-to-day basis. Tom was the director of the group. Jim provided tactical skills, techniques and practices as it pertained to treasury functions. Tom was the big picture guy. We talked about different areas of the company, people in the finance 'food chain' and growth opportunities. The overall mission I had for the two years on the program was to learn as much as I could, create value within each group, produce great products and make an impression with leadership. When it was time for me to transition out of Treasury, the program director was selling me on the most undesirable rotational assignment. Our MBA class had six members. The class that entered Chevron the year before had five members. Thus, eleven MBAs would fulfill the rotational assignments. We talked amongst ourselves, shared perspectives, compared notes and knew the premium versus bad rotational assignments. I knew that the program director was trying to sell me a lemon, but Tom came to the rescue. He and Jim were Finance Development Program alumni and Tom was a company 'darling'. I gently and matter-of-factly shared the possibility of me being placed in the weak rotational assignment and he immediately hopped on the phone with the program director to squash the deal. The assignment was given to a young lady that eventually left the company within a few months of being on that assignment. As a result of my support-members, I was able to avoid that situation. Fortunately, I was not the wrong guy this time.

My second and third rotations were equally rewarding with respect to the work, but the mentorship quotient diminished. My second rotation was with the Chevron Shipping Company. My job was to fully leverage thirty-two vessels that Chevron utilized to carry its cargo. And when there was no Chevron cargo to transport, I had to find other cargo to ship and make a profit. The puzzle solving sensibilities appealed to my obsessive compulsive disorder to think, explore, create, solve and do something again and again. I thought my learning and understanding jumped exponentially as this rotation was a staple for the program. The setting was an office for two where it was a collaborative work environment with a junior executive a few years removed from the program, coaching a new program member. My junior executive Lee was exceptional as he would spit out rates, travel routes, vessels and all things shipping without any interruption to what he was doing. He was a marvelous partner to have until I came in on a Monday and thought I had done something wrong. I had been working on a financial work up on a Suez Canal deal for multiple vessels and I thought I had screwed up. My manager Tom, not Tom from Treasury, closed the door. He shared that both he and Lee were heading to the Chevron London office. Of course, I was happy for those guys as that's what this game is about, moving onward and upward. At that point, both guys were kind of checked out. I struggled after that in the assignment. I needed Lee's quick knowledge of rates, routes, analytic techniques and Tom's experienced insight and lead blocking with executives. As I recall, my new boss had little sympathy for me losing my office mate and manager. He showed no mercy with respect to my overall assignment review and how I ranked with other MBAs that had served time in the Chevron Shipping Company. The narrative was unlike my summer internship and Treasury evaluations. I took the assessment and feedback in stride. I thought it was unfair, but this was the real world. This was Corporate America. I did not have a counter response for maintaining the momentum in a changing work environment. I did not insulate myself from a fiery new boss that did not look at effort, activity or bad circumstances as his focus was on results, achievement and the delivery of results. He could have shown more understanding, remorse or provided more tools and learning for our success. No system or privilege at work here, simply an acute case of an ism...rectumism.

Before my Shipping rotation was complete, I had lunch with Tom in Treasury to suggest he politic on my behalf to the program director for a New York assignment on Chevron's commodities trading desk. He did so, but I was not awarded the rotation for many reasons. Once again, it was not the right time or situation and I was not the right guy. I was disappointed, which led to me not agreeing in an immature way, but I trusted Tom so I kept it moving and did not press the program director for the assignment. I eventually was assigned to the Chevron Overseas Company. My job was to manage African and European business unit production and financial reporting. It was essentially an accounting gig that included numerous weekly, monthly and quarterly reports. My guy Dollar Bill was a member of this organization so I had the job learned in no time. The game changer in this assignment was when I had a lengthy conversation with a Chevron colleague in Angola. This was before 'the cloud' and the myriad of financial software packages. I uncovered that my colleague and I were producing similar reports and that the information flowing my way was actually produced by him. I had the same conversation with another colleague in Europe. As a result of our information sharing, I was able to do reporting significantly quicker and add more value from an analytical point of view. I gained favor from some of my teammates and it created similar inquiries and mining for information from other international business units. These probes created systemic enhancements to our group's standard operating procedures. As a

Finance Development Program member, I was on the radar of the president and we had a few memorable planned and impromptu lunches where he elevated my awareness and thinking regarding the entire business unit and how my group's reports were used to guide the business. When my time was complete with the Overseas Group, my learning, knowledge, accounting skills, production and financial acumen had increased immensely. The positive momentum was back on course until during my final evaluation, my manager 'punched me in the mouth' with two dings: (1) He shared that my choice of dress was too upscale for the group. For real? This was part of my evaluation? You shared this after 6 - 7 months? The dress code was casual, but when I dressed casually at Chevron for some odd reason, my co-workers would ask me mailroom or maintenance questions, so I couldn't dress casually like the typical white guy at the job. I understood that most of the mailroom and maintenance guys are Black, but I do have a distinctive look regardless of what I wear. I was not a big proponent of casual dress and oftentimes exercised the optional shirt and tie. (2) I was too 'cool'. The nature of the job was hitting deadlines and delivering in completion with accuracy and a high degree of excellence. The culture was somewhat of a frenzied environment when deadlines were upon us. I did not prescribe to conveying pressure, exemplifying stress or sharing the difficulties of the job. I put my head down, did the work and got the job done. I understood the ideas of fitting in, going along and that stream of thinking. It was just odd that there was more evaluation, assessment and coaching emphasis on my apparel choices and image and very little with respect to my analytical shortcomings or work production. Sadly, the personal stuff is ALWAYS in play in Corporate America and at top spots at companies. I experienced this for 20 years. Folks choose likeability over capability. If they like you, they will cover for you, hide your weaknesses and keep others on the fringe so there is no comparison. It was a weird exit from that group. I was certain that I would not be returning soon to that situation, as I was the wrong guy for this group and definitely for that particular manager.

My fourth and final rotation was in Chevron's Corporate Strategy Group. I had the honor of performing financial analyses for Dave O'Reilly who later became Chevron's CEO. My manager Bob was truly a gem. He was hard-nosed, smart, understood various areas of the company and was a strong finance professional. The work was gratifyingly challenging, and Bob was a hard charger that focused on every word and every number when presenting our findings, point of view and analysis to Dave. Bob was not the ladder climbing or MBA type professional. I remember him as being a grinder who cared about the work and not the other corporate stuff, which I appreciated. He actually let me shine a few times on work projects when he was the mastermind behind the projects. It was kind of like, 'do your thing kid' gestures. We worked on briefing Dave on Enron Corporation's business model, the source of its revenues and a meeting with its former CEO Ken Lay. The work also encompassed the financial gains of Chevron partnering with McDonalds as a gas station retail partner, Chevron acquiring Texaco, and the pros and cons of a multimillion dollar acquisition of a small chemical company. This was all great learning and work effort for me. My rotation was complete, and this was the last piece of my corporate finance puzzle. The only thing in the balance and in question during this rotation was my first full-time position with the company rolling off the program.

I obtained counsel from Tom in Treasury, Dollar Bill, Marty and Greg on my next move. Tom had shared an opportunity with me to be selected for a '28 Days On and 28 Days Off' expatriate job in Kazakhstan. The job was sweet on paper with increased pay, 28 days of work and 28 days off, a round trip ticket to and from Kazakhstan; and to any place in the world every month. Free housing accommodations with paid meals and other nice perks that came with the job. It was a dream job for anyone worthy of selection. It was an understatement to say I was hyped on the job. He shared that there was discussion to diversify the expatriate staff due to the grueling nature of the assignment and polarizing weather conditions of extreme heat and cold. Literally, some of the older workers were getting drastically ill and dying. After talking to Tom, I consulted Dollar Bill. He confirmed that there was discussion about getting younger staffers. He was more forthright and brutal, stating that the old white guys need to step aside, forgo the money and let the young turks carry the torch. Dollar Bill had done a 28/28 assignment in Angola and knew the rigors of the assignment, less the extreme weather conditions that affect everything in terms of the overall conditions of the work and dormitory sites. I smelled blood in the water so I had to use a 'silver bullet'. I arranged to meet with Marty Klitten, Chevron's CFO. He had been a huge supporter of the program as he was at the top of the finance food chain. Marty also periodically had meetings with the other Black men in the program. The year before me, three of the five in that class had been Black men. Two of the Black men did not make it off the program, as they found better opportunities elsewhere. In one case, there was a total lack of respect from the treasurer. Marty and I met about Kazakhstan. Marty, who as CFO could make a unilateral decision, was tepid and timid during our conversation. The year prior, he reversed a decision to not hire the one remaining Black program member to be on a SAP Implementation Team after his stint on the program, which made him the first Black man to advance from the program in nearly 20 years. I was hoping that Marty would make the call on Kazakhstan but my chances were 50/50. After a week or so, Tom shared that the opportunity would not materialize for me. Tom, the consummate professional, well-balanced cool guy, said all the right things to pacify me. I was still hot. There was always talk about the benefits of the program, the leadership training, skill development, diversity, best and brightest getting opportunities, blah, blah, blah. But when it came down to action, it was the same old game, I didn't get the position. My Dollar Bill confirmed it was some system, ism and privilege bullcrap.

With that disappointment, I turned my sights on the Pension Fund Management group. I had an affinity for investments and strategy. I discussed the job with the program director. He did not think it was a good fit. His rationale was lightweight, vague and I was not truly convinced it was a bad fit. It was not favorable to my pursuit of the job, as the program director served as the procurer of full-time jobs for program participants. This dilemma required finesse and savvy. I connected with my guy Greg to get insights and strategy. Greg was unaware that the process for securing a full-time job following the program was dependent on the program manager. He also shared that the head of the Pension Fund Management group was a guy people were afraid of. He was smarter than the smart guys, did what he did extremely and phenomenally well, did not play politics and was not the friendly, bubbly guy that the executives prefer in their circle. Most of all, Greg shared that Neil was impossible to figure out. Greg believed that all of this probably gave the program director some level of pause in approaching Neil. Make no mistake, Greg was diplomatic with a cut throat mentality. He coached me to 'go for the kill'. Since I had not met Neil in my two years on the program, Greg suggested that I meet with him one-on-one to discuss the possibility of me being a part of his group. Soon After, I arranged a lunch meeting with Neil. He was a bring-my-own-lunch-from-home type of guy, but on that day his assistant shared with me his favorite sandwich spot in San Francisco and lunch was on me. Given his legendary history, one would have thought he was 7 feet tall and breathed fire. We had a pretty good discussion. At the top of the hour, I had convinced my Michigan Investments Class professor to call Neil and speak on my behalf. As Neil accepted the call, I made my exit. Long story short, Neil offered me a job to join his group.

Neil was and is by far the best boss I ever had. He stretched my thinking as well as my financial and investment strategy acumen. He was tough and similar to a powerful teacher or coach. And, I never wanted to let Neil down by giving him less than my best. His accountability bar was the highest I had experienced and I operated higher than I ever had in the past. When I joined, the investment team within the group was a team of two with Neil leading the way. I was the low man on the totem pole so I did the grunt work such as gathering data, performing preliminary financial work-ups before I submitted to the senior analyst Ken. Then, collectively we would make final decisions. Ken was sharp, a great teacher and had mastered the art of quantitative assessing risk factors on MS Excel spreadsheets. I had to take a class and work overtime just to keep up with him. Some things cannot be taught and you have to simply learn through experience. I had to quickly combine my MBA investment learnings, real world scenarios and spreadsheet formulas to talk Ken and Neil's language. The bulk of our work was assessing institutional fund managers' performance independently and measuring how that performance would be maximized within our portfolio of other fund managers. Also, we managed an internal real estate investment portfolio that also needed to be managed for return on investment versus risk. Our group also advised other international Chevron subsidiaries and finance groups on return on investment analytics. The latter was basically finance executives respecting Neil's intellect and wanting his approval on any major decisions.

 I thought the job was dynamic and exciting. I had *Investor Business Daily* delivered to my home and I would read it on the Bay Area Rapid Transit (BART) train to work. When I arrived at the office, I would read *The Wall Street Journal*. *Investor Business Daily* was more so about market behavior. I read *The Wall Street Journal* for the culture, commentary and news of the companies and people influencing the market. I spent most of my days watching *Reuters*, *Bloomberg* and Chevron portfolio monitors determining how assets will be positioned based on market occurrences and trends as well as currency shifts. Early in my stint in the group, I worked primarily with Ken. He was the guy that was responsible for sharpening my skill sets. He always had me ready and prepared for Neil. And, you had to literally be ready for Neil. I have never encountered another executive who knew essentially everything about everything with respect to the business of Pension Fund Management. Neil is the kind of guy that you could give a 10 page report full of numbers and he would spot the four numbers that were incorrect. I am talking about assumptions, input errors, bad formulas, whatever…Neil was on it. And, 99 times out of 100 times he was correct. The cool thing about Neil is that he would not beat you up about the error or mistake. He actually crystalized my definition of error versus mistake. As I reflect, he did not mind a few errors but he was less tolerable of mistakes. He was a well balanced guy but you could tell when he was disgusted, satisfied or pleased. I embraced sharing my point of view with him and making a recommendation and hearing him shred it or endorse it. I learned through encounters with Neil how to quickly sharpen my game to elevate to his level of efficacy.

After about 8 months in the group, Ken received a promotion and moved to Houston. Neil shared that I would assume his responsibilities and he would determine if we would need to bring another person to backfill my position. I recall a conversation around additional compensation but not a promotion or band level bump per se. But I was all in on stepping up. The best benefit I can remember is that I would sit in on meetings with Neil as well as be in his stead when he could not, or chose not to, attend meetings. I was eating up the intelligence around the operational aspects of fund management as well as sharpening my decision making acumen. Neil was pretty cunning as well. He had a myriad of tricks and head games he would play on internal and external executives. Nothing divisive, dishonest, in poor taste or the like, but just self-entertaining antics. I understood it. Neil was just on a whole other level and he needed peculiar stuff to keep him interested. As I got to know Neil more, I began to watch his every move and ask him more questions. He showed no pause in engaging me all the time regardless of the inquiry. One day, there was a letter on my desk stating I had received a pay increase and maybe even a promotion. I immediately headed over to Neil's office. I recall the first thing Neil said was, "I am thinking about letting you go". He was all smiles and I realized this letter was a good thing. He shared that I had done such a great job in Ken's absence that he would not be hiring a third person. Damn, I was Neil's guy. It was a wonderful feeling. Without question, it was the right time, the right situation, and I was the right guy.

After serving in the Pension Fund Management group for about two years, an opportunity arose to essentially be the lead finance guy in Bermuda for Chevron. This is a scripted position that for as long as anyone could remember was held by a Finance Development Program participant. I knew the current person in the role and he believed I was an ideal candidate in terms of interest level and experience. Neil signed off on me pursuing the job and Marty and Greg knew of my interest. I thought I was a shoe in for the job. I was definitely counting my chickens before they hatched. Keeping my options open, at the request of a close Michigan friend Gerry, who was the east coast marketing lead for Nike, I applied to be the newly minted marketing lead for the west coast. I did not have marketing experience but the interviews went well enough for me to garner legitimate consideration.

One Tuesday, I was having lunch with a colleague in the Treasury group. I mentioned that I was waiting for the decision on the Bermuda job. She shared that she had read that the job had already been filled. We immediately went to her office and rummaged through her recycle bin. As she had claimed, the job had been filled. I was glad to see that Neil was not on the communique so he probably was not aware the job had been filled. I was a 6' 1" towering white hot inferno...probably the hottest I had been in my life. I simply placed the crumpled up notice on Neil's desk and went home. On Wednesday, I received a call from Nike extending me a job offer. We hammered out the details and I submitted my resignation to Neil on

Monday morning. Of course, there was conversation about me over-reacting but I was resolved in my decision.

I gave everyone at Chevron an audience that wanted to talk me out of my decision. Marty's conversation was the most impactful and insightful. He shared for the first time in the history of that assignment that the decision was to hire a Bermuda national. We also had a real talk about the Kazakhstan hiring practices. As he looked at my file, he said "Damon, you are doing very well here...and you're Black. Ken is even one of your supports." NOTE: Ken was the CEO at the time. I was invited by Ken to accompany him to Los Angeles for a business trip. Corporate jet, face time, hobnobbing, rubbing elbows, etc. I did not take offense to the Black reference. Marty was one of those executives that wanted to see me, other Black people and women do well, but he did not want to disrupt the privilege of the white guys at Chevron. Marty was full disclosure with respect to where the company was in terms of diversity and my advancement potential. He had high expectations of Chevron getting to the mountaintop of fairness and equality one day, but that would involve me lowering my expectations of fairness and equality. I chose to change companies and industries to be treated fairly with a real opportunity to rise. At the time, my experience at Chevron was the best for me in many ways. It was and is a phenomenal company in terms of development, training and taking care of its people, and I do mean its people. No remorse or hate, I just was not one of those people, which made the situation, timing and everything wrong.

Key Takeaways

- When you are in a fiercely competitive environment, you must be highly qualified along with having a little something extra in terms of style, experience or charisma. And, sometimes, the qualifications don't matter because the key decision makers prefer the 'something extra'. Keep it moving, as this is not always the case.

- It gets really tricky at major institutions and in Corporate America. Always seek out truth tellers. You might not like what you hear, but at least you know the facts that make up the story. Over time, you will appreciate the truth.

- Sometimes the grass is greener on the other side. Constantly have real talks with yourself in terms of what you will accept, tolerate and choose to deal with in work and in life. At times, you simply reach your limit and must move on. Other times, you may choose to endure. Above all, make it your choice.

6

The Swoosh Life

> *Money, shoes, product, sponsorships? That's nothing. The real value is to be able to leverage the brand.*
> – RALPH GREENE, VP NIKE SPORTS MARKETING

You may be wondering, how does an Economics major with a MBA in Finance go from managing a pension fund to becoming the Head of Marketing for Nike in the #2 market in the USA? It probably was the systems, isms or privilege, right? Not at all. Let's rewind. I didn't mention earlier that my high school homeboy Lonnie, who was all in on going to college, was also the school DJ. He was ahead of his time when it came to the use of music at basketball and football games as well as making school social events hot. I took note of this, loving the energy he created. It may not mean much now since everyone has a mobile phone, but back then Lonnie owned a camera. This was huge, as most families in my neighborhood did not own one. It meant that he was creating content, selfies and 'back shots' before they were popular. In short, he was Mr. Cool. My other ace buddy, and sometimes business partner Lou, who I knew since junior high, drove a Porsche and had a wardrobe probably more valuable than most of our teachers' yearly salary. I saw the game they were running, and this would heavily influence my marketing tactics in the future.

Building the Early Brand Legacy of Nike

When I was making my way through Cal, it was not all about the books. My roomie and frat buddy, Earnie aka East Coast Sears, and frat line brother Eddie aka Sweet Lou was like a spice rack. Those brothas had so much flavor! It was inevitable that I was going to learn and hold on to some of it. Both were on the Cal Basketball team. Eddie was a fashionista and playboy. Earnie was a triple threat because he was a hooper, rapper and dancer. I went to school in Berkeley but lived in Oakland. Berkeley was your typical all white college town with a blend of academics and youthful spirit. On the other hand, Oakland was a predominately Black, blue collar city and rebellious. I gravitated to Oakland due to the familiar feel and its edginess. I felt like I was back home in South Central.

At Michigan, my roomie Ron was the Black Business Students Association president. Guess who he assigned to be the head of Social Events? We partied responsibly. I also interned for the athletic department working as an Associate Athletic Director. I was able to be 'in the mix' when Desmond Howard won the Heisman Award and when the Fab 5 took the world by storm. Wow! Magical times just thinking about how crazy and hyped it was on campus. When I returned to the Bay, I was building my social network and staying plugged in to movers and shakers by serving as a leader in Phi Beta Sigma Fraternity and the National Black MBA Association in Oakland and San Francisco chapters respectively. I also worked closely with a creative agency and a rap record label that afforded me insights into the ever-growing world and culture of hip hop. These companies and their dynamic leaders exposed me to the likes of MC Hammer, Too $hort, E-40, Master P as well as other rappers and R&B singers popular in the Bay Area...along with the means, ways and habits within the music, culture and business. Thus, I was not exactly a 'bean counter' or a novice to sports, influencers, marketing and moving the needle at retail. I had credentials that Nike respected along with a unique set of skills that Nike appreciated.

The first couple of months at Nike was somewhat overwhelming. It was a new job, a new industry, and a new position, with no staff and an empty office. In addition, my boss Jon was located 1000 miles away. I traveled to the Nike World Headquarters in Oregon, learned a lot about the company and met many people. But my job had no playbook, no how-to manual, no script or anything as a reference from the past. Everything was brand new. During my early visits to Nike WHQ, I received the best perspective on the job from our department head Ralph. I showed Ralph my 90 Day Plan. He chuckled, handed it back to me and said, "Look, I need you to handle and stay on top of everything Nike west of Texas." And there it was, that was the job. The daunting task to ignite the Nike Brand in the Western United States was humongous. It also appealed to my obsession and desire to change the game in all ways possible. I then hustled to learn everything about Nike west of Texas including but not limited to retailers, ad campaigns, athletes under contract, professional franchise deals, key relationships, everything. Slowly but surely, I began to understand the 'Nike Footprint', tactics and strategies west of Texas, but mainly in San Francisco and Los Angeles. I began to create my own organizational chart of internal and external individuals influencing the Nike business in my region. It was such a huge job, I knew I needed help... and fast.

Nike was a relatively young company and daring the world to tell it to slow down. All things Nike was about 'Just Do It' and it fit my mentality at the time. Within 3 months in my position, Jon was able to provide me with a 'stretch assignment' working at the 1996 Summer Olympics in Atlanta. It was a once in a lifetime opportunity that provided me with invaluable experience and exposure. I was assigned to the Nike Olympic Park, which was the premier location for tourists, global spectators, sports dignitaries and the 'who's who' descending on Atlanta. It served as Nike's hub for its iconic athletes and premium product as well as an authentic, engaging sports experience. The other perks I received included all access to all things Nike such as the athletes,

VIP Lounges and tickets to events. I could not have written a better script for this amazing experience. I was able to study the game plan of a global marketing campaign, experiential marketing activation, retail pop program, athlete deployment and brand statement. The Atlanta Olympic experience set the stage and built the foundation for what I would build in my region. Upon my return to Los Angeles, I began searching for a 'partner in crime'. I was desperately searching to hire someone that balanced my skill set, who knew Los Angeles from top to bottom and was a 'sports guy'. I struck up a conversation on the set of a Nike commercial with my friend Nigel. He was the owner of a casting agency, a heavyweight basketball consulting firm, and he was plugged into elite circles. He recommended I speak with one of his fellow UCLA Bruin alumni, Thaddeus. I met with Thaddeus soon after, and we became partners. It was one of the best decisions I ever made.

Thaddeus was born and raised in Los Angeles and graduated from UCLA. While at UCLA, he was the team manager of the basketball team. His pedigree and temperament were perfect; this combination was just what I was looking for. Thaddeus was the executive director and coach of an elite youth basketball program. Over the years, his players included Hall of Fame candidates and NBA Champions Paul Pierce and Kevin Garnett as well as NBA players Baron Davis, Gilbert Arenas and Milton Palacio and a host of players that attended NCAA, Power 5 Conference colleges. He understood the streets, basketball, sports and business. I just needed him to understand me, and over time he did. The other piece of the staffing puzzle was Jerry. I had returned to Los Angeles after a national marketing meeting in New York. I realized that in order for the Western Region to be Nike's #1 marketing group in the USA, we needed more muscle. In sharing the profile of my needs to my creative agency lead Daven, he recommended I interview Jerry. He was sharp, thoughtful, smart and an amenable dude. His father was a former boxer, so Jerry also had a sports pedigree and understood certain nuances of the sport's world.

Between my mad scientist approach to marketing, Thaddeus' tactical knowledge and Jerry's 'get it done' drive, we made a formidable team. We definitely were up to the task of doing damage to the LA sports scene.

As our team began to build in-house properties, cut deals with local sports league directors and form partnerships with youth sports governing bodies, we quickly hit our stride. In addition to our local initiatives, we also were responsible for leveraging NFL, NBA, WNBA, NHL and MLS league deals. During this time, there was an emergence of Niketown openings in key west coast markets that we were looking to strategize around. And of course, there were a myriad of shoe launches that we needed to support. The plans, work and wins were rapid fire. The advertising campaigns, the footwear and apparel design, the presence at retail and most of all the culture was all in your face. It was ingenious fueled with rebellious tones which was perfect positioning for the brand. We were able to build programming that marketed the sport and product categories, specific footwear and athletes. Some of our naming conventions were Swoosh, Flight and Uptempo League, Supreme Challenge, School of Skillz, Represent, Real Run, Heart & Soul Challenge to name a few.
The other competitive advantage we had was that we were young Black guys that understood the intersection of hip hop culture, sports and lifestyle. We had a great feel for what the people wanted from messaging, from a creative design realm and programming standpoint. Whenever Thaddeus, Jerry, and I showed up anytime and anywhere, the stakes were elevated because 'The Nike Guys' were in the house. Yes, we had management teams sitting in Beaverton, Oregon that had power and point of view, but we had the ability to turn the seeds of a corporate-driven idea into an oak tree. We had the 'secret sauce' to turn a national initiative into a campaign that felt worthy of street credibility. And, we remained true to Ralph's mantra; we handled everything west of Texas.

Nike was uber competitive and the environment was sports-like: aggressive and cocky. The vast majority of former athletes were intelligent folks. Whenever there were questions in terms of branding, direction, position and/or stances, the right move was to align with the athlete, culture or artist. Also, this was the 90s, hip hop was in full swing and was taking over the hearts and minds of millennials, influencers and people all over the world. The powers that be at Nike were smart and nimble enough to adapt to the world of hip hop as its athletes were connected to the culture and all things around it. The marketing organization had morphed as well. I was no longer reporting to Jon and Ralph. Jon transitioned out of Nike and formed his own marketing agency. Ralph was still at Nike seeking, signing and serving world class athletes. There was also more engagement on a management and creative agency level. As a result, within a few years at Nike, I reported to four different managers with three residing in Beaverton and one in Orange County, which is a suburb of Los Angeles. As with most subjective jobs, there are a few philosophical conflicts.

At Nike, I would say that I was aligned with management 80% of the time. The 20% misalignment was on engagement and expression of culture. My first encounter where I had to directly oppose management was Nike's East vs West campaign. This campaign was embedded in basketball street legends, icon basketball courts and NYC vs LA style of hoop. However, there was a bigger and dangerous East vs West battle happening in rap with Bad Boy Entertainment and Death Row Records. Hip hop media circles were pitting P Diddy and Notorious BIG against Suge Knight and Tupac. Nike's ad agency crafted the East vs. West campaign and was striving to 'double down' on it by amplifying the elements of the campaign in New York and Los Angeles. One of the G.O.A.Ts in advertising, Soul Brotha #1 Jimmy was leading the agency's charge. I was summoned to be in the room along with my NYC counterpart Lincoln and some ancillary functional leads that would be vital to the success of the campaign. A few months before, I had met Jimmy for the first time. He was pitching another ad campaign and whipped out Parliament Funkadelic album covers to tell and convey the storyline. I loved it. In all my years in Corporate America I had never experienced real talk and in-depth cultural secrets shared to 'sell' an idea. Jimmy was masterful. However, with his East vs West campaign, I was not buying it. Lincoln was not either. I could not speak for Bad Boy Entertainment, but that Death Row Records life was real and not just media hype. Death Row Records had deep ties to real killers and this East vs West thing was like claiming gang sets with all the elements of gunplay and violence. NYC marketing lead, Lincoln chimed in with perspective because he formerly worked at Bad Boy Entertainment. He confirmed that it would not be wise to roll out the campaign. The management team was looking to us, the guys in the street, the frontliners for advice. We killed the campaign. Jimmy was hot. I can still feel him. He thought we were 'selling out'. I saw Jimmy not too long ago and he still thinks we did. I laughed it off. The cool thing about this situation was that the subject matter experts, meaning us brothers who were culture mavens and sports guys, were able to sit around a table, discuss the pros and cons, assess a situation, come to a consensus and the Nike System was able to respond accordingly. The campaigns and programs still lived, and lived well, we just killed the elements we thought were dangerous, but that would not always be the case.

I was fortunate to see the development of the marketing offices in New York, Chicago and Atlanta in addition to building a presence in Los Angeles. There were great exchanges of best practices in terms of sports, retail and culture as each region had its own. Oftentimes, those nuances of the marketplace were totally missed by our management teams in Beaverton, who were ultimately calling the shots. After all, the world of sports, athletes, music, art, culture and all the elements that made great brands were rapidly changing at light speed. And we have to remember, all this was happening before

Instagram, Twitter, Tik Tok, Youtube and Google, so you could not stay glued to your mobile phone and learn culture. You had to be in it, connect to it, feel it, embrace it, and be authentic with it.

The Air Jordan Effect

One major project I was asked to consult on was the launch of the Jordan Brand. Contrary to popular 'hood belief', Michael Jordan did not break away from Nike to launch Jordan. The Jordan Brand was and is a subsidiary of Nike, Inc. The first employee of the Jordan Brand was a young, sharp, enterprising, big thinker named Erin. As I would often do with fellow Nike employees, I gave Erin a full breakdown of the Los Angeles sports vibe, lifestyle flow, influencers, etc. We spent a day strategizing on how to launch the Jordan Brand in Los Angeles. At the time, the west coast was familiar with the first batch of Jordan Athletes, in particular Eddie Jones with the Lakers. After our face-to-face visit, I served as a thought partner to Erin on his full rollout plan. We connected at sales meetings, Nike WHQ and regional and national events. I thought that his approach and thinking was placing him, the Jordan Brand and my region to successfully launch the brand. During a planning meeting with my manager at the time, we were reviewing the retail distribution placement for the Jordan product as well as our seeding plan, which outlines key people that would receive the newly released product. My manager scoffed at the idea of seeding Jordan products with barbers and merchandising barbershops with Jordan Brand creative. I was mystified. I had been deploying this strategy at my own barber and barbershop and I know the heat it created. I am sure Thaddeus, Jerry and a number of Black employees at Nike were doing the same thing. There was even a Nike ad campaign with basketball legends in a barbershop that was hugely successful and well received. I could not believe the reaction to something so culturally relevant, extremely effective and innovative was seen as a poor utilization of budget, time and resource deployment.

This conversation sparked other uses of funds, focus of marketing strategies that extended further than traditional media and corporate techniques. On the low, I supported the urban marketing tactics Erin deployed and the Jordan Brand launch was a huge success in Los Angeles. We were able to impact the marketplace with the traditional approaches that made management happy but we were also able to add a little flavor that we knew the people in the streets would connect to and appreciate. My key learning in working with Erin, the Jordan Brand and my local management was there were limits to where Nike Inc would go in terms of fully leveraging the culture, non-entertainment and athlete influencers and the usage of non-traditional marketing activations. This project and my work with Erin would serve as a turning point in my thinking about the future of marketing brands, sports, products and lifestyles.

In my corner of the world, I was enjoying the Swoosh Life. I was building sports properties in Los Angeles and San Francisco, developing co-marketing campaigns and seasonal activations with the Lakers, Raiders, Sparks and Galaxy. I was working with an array of professional athletes that worked and lived in LA as well as creating retail sell-through programs with urban and regional accounts. I then decided to approach my counterparts in New York, Chicago and Atlanta to support a program that would provide local heat on the street as well as bolster our might nationally as a team and brand. The campaign was called 'Represent'. It was essentially a tournament that ended the debate of who had the best basketball squad in the major markets in the USA. Each region would conduct a local tournament with the winners being awarded a weekend in LA to battle it out on the world-famous Venice Beach courts. My organization hosted the weekend and all the other teams in any region had to do was land at LAX, as we took care of the rest. Other than that, the battle had to be settled on the court. Kudos to my team and the entire LA Nike office. From our Sales Team, Entertainment Marketing, Niketown LA to our 'Nike Family', we provided a magnificent, fun-filled and highly competitive weekend for about 100 of the country's best non-NBA and non-NCAA basketball players. The championship game was scheduled the same time as Game 3 of the NBA Finals pitting Michael Jordan and the Bulls against the Utah Jazz. I had always been nervous about the timing of our championship game and the NBA Finals. We took the chance that the stands would not be empty and it would still be an epic moment in LA Basketball. I was nervous until I saw the stands at Venice Beach packed with local hoop fans. Our partners for the event included two record labels, a beverage company, a local quick service restaurant and a radio station. In addition, we hired a street team despite management's pause on such guerrilla tactics. Ralph's mantra always stuck and continued to stick in my head, "Ask for forgiveness, not permission." I knew we had really created a ripple effect when someone from Earvin 'Magic' Johnson's office called and requested I reserve a row for him and his guests. We had a celebrity game as the prelude to the Represent Championship so there were tons of fans at the game as well. Magic was kind enough to congratulate the fellas and perform the opening tip. What, Magic Johnson at the game, providing sound bites, conducting the opening tip?! And not to mention the ambiance and culture merge of hoops, waves, beautiful people, music and the Venice Beach stands and boardwalk packed together? High fives all around. We had overachieved for real.

The same weekend as Represent, there was a skatepark dedication in San Diego. Management decided to attend those festivities but they did arrive in time to experience Represent as well. Following Represent in Los Angeles, there was a national marketing meeting in Beaverton a few days later. The head of the department shared that we should meet before I left Beaverton. I was presumptuous and thought he would commend me on a job well done on Represent. Nope! I was told that Represent was a poor representation of the Nike Brand. The explanation was puzzling but at the same time clear.

Management did not understand street team battles, cyphers, outdoor high-level streetball, rap music, hip hop culture and entertainment all coming together in one location being enjoyed in tandem. Management did not know what they were experiencing. As we discussed the decision, I truly understood the rationale. I did not agree, but it would have taken too many words, too much time and too much correcting to refute some of the assessments. After all, management is management.

Essentially, I was told that the program should not be included in my annual marketing plan and that I needed to develop another concept. Surprisingly, even to myself, I was not angry or the like. I knew I had to pivot. My marketing colleagues in New York, Chicago and Atlanta were stunned. We were unified in our thoughts that Represent was groundbreaking for the basketball category, region, brand, athletes and influencers. More importantly, it was the biggest coordinated national program that united us and brought us together...oh well. Similar to my thoughts pursuant to the Jordan Brand launch, I knew that there were some strategic shortcomings emanating from the marketing leadership team at Nike WHQ. I perceived this as a unique opportunity for me to fill a void of some sort. Within a year of this incident, I would transition from Nike to form my own marketing agency.

Key Takeaways

- Brands are different from businesses. Don't be fooled, lured or misguided by consumer-facing campaigns, marketing and advertising. Study leadership and how those people operate, which will indicate how you will be measured, promoted and advanced while working on such campaigns.

- Use your position to advance yourself. Do not simply do the work, do you! Your position should be an exchange where you are giving your skills and learning or gaining something in return. If you get hired, then allow all of your talents, gifts and abilities to be on full display. Not for them, but for you.

- Always make note of what is hot and what is not. Do not find yourself working on irrelevant projects, tasks or the like. Be in the epicenter of critical and vital work within your group, business, company, etc. to stay on top of your craft.

I'm a child of the 70s. I always mimicked black movie heroes. This was my middle school graduation.

Always helps to have protectors in your life from the start. My big brother Eric and sister Elaine.

Top: Moms and I during my Cal graduation weekend. Proud moment for the entire family.

I was always a great hitter. Focus, see the ball, drive through it. I could hit the curveball, too... literally and figuratively.

Magic Johnson has always been a great leader. He showed me the way to entrepreneurship.

My first of many trips to Barcelona. This time with 'Half Man, Half Amazing', 'Vinsanity' Vince Carter.

Great conversation with Kobe around his 4th Championship, his sweetest! It was one of Kobe's missions to beat out Shaq in championship records. Mission Accomplished.

I was part of about 20 Michael Jordan Flight Schools in Santa Barbara and Las Vegas. MJ is my favorite icon...fun, sh$% talker, approachable, one of the guys.

The signature DHaley forward lean. Rolling with LeBron at his King for Kid's Bikeathon in Akron, OH. No one has done more for his city than LBJ. Kudos to him.

Dominique Wilkins 'The Human Highlight Reel'. Great times at the Naismith Hall of Fame Ceremony.

DH Baobei in Shanghai. I was gifted a 'chop'. It still remains one of my greatest moments as a professional. Great work, great people, great adventure.

Rooftop party after a job well done. Celebrating with Patricia, Adam in the back and Glory with the cigars.

My pops and I. The bucket hat, shades, gold chain and cigar was his thing. Miss him dearly.

Diann Valentine and me. "Ike and Tina, Marie and Donnie, Ashford and Simpson, Clyde and Bonnie" from "Bonnie & Clyde Theme" by Ice Cube and YoYo

Doesn't get better than this, Riann, Diann and I. Our first wedding day, followed by three more.

My youngest niece Sierra got me good. We always have fun celebrating life.

7

The U

> *Trends come and go, but cool is forever...*
> – STEVE STOUTE, FOUNDER
> TRANSLATION ADVERTISING AGENCY

After figuring out that there was a greater opportunity to build vast, in-depth marketing strategies that leveraged the emergence of hip hop culture, micro-influencers and urban lifestyles, I began thinking around what my next move would look like. My four year run with Nike was more like an eight year career in the rest of the business world. I had been able to be an intricate part of many new ventures for Nike since everything the company and my region did was fertile ground to grow the business in a new frontier. Similar to my Chevron experience, I was able to learn so much in a short amount of time. It was truly an amazing eight year journey to accumulate finance, marketing, advertising, creative development and marketplace acumen at two corporations that were global industry leaders. Pursuant to Represent being shut down, I began to seed the idea that I was looking for an opportunity outside of Nike. The Nike Brand had become invincible and I was identified as 'The Nike Guy' so people could not fathom that I would be looking to transition. Then, one day I received a call from Magic Johnson Enterprises.

DAMON HALEY

A Loss Can Be a Signal You're on the Right Path

The big man wanted to meet with me. I had interacted with Earvin on several occasions both personally and professionally. To be honest, I thought the meeting would entail some type of sponsorship for one of his companies or events. Whatever the context of the meeting was, when Earvin calls, you simply ask when and where. When I arrived at his office, I was instructed to wait in the main conference room. I was there alone until suddenly people filled the conference room, puzzled at my presence. A cake was brought in and candles were lit. I was a bit uncomfortable but rolled with the punches. A young lady was escorted in and everyone sang 'Happy Birthday'. Of course, I joined in. There was the usual small talk, thank you chatter and happy birthday wishes to the young lady. When the staff exited the room, Earvin was delighted at the awkwardness of me being part of a stranger's celebration but commended me for taking everything in stride.

We took our seats around the board room table and we were joined by 3 to 4 staff members. Earvin began to discuss the business operations of Magic Johnson Enterprises and shared that he wanted me to join the team. I was totally caught off guard. Earvin did all the talking but his team members were engaged and attentive. I knew a few of them so the energy was supportive, optimistic and there were smiles all around. It was a great conversation and I was honored Earvin thought so highly of me. We scheduled a follow up meeting to provide me time to think about the opportunity and come back with any questions, curiosities, etc. And, I sure did. I showed up with three pages of notes and seventeen questions. Earvin was incredibly gracious with his time. We met for a couple of hours and he answered every question about his businesses, his 25 year and $25 million Lakers deals, Converse contract, relationship with Dr. Buss, his org chart, future aspirations, everything. To this day, it was one of my greatest meetings. Over the next week or so, I met with a few more people on his staff including his right hand guy Ken, who

I was equally impressed with as he was a monster deal maker and real estate baron.

As time progressed after the series of meetings, I never received any follow-up from Magic Johnson Enterprises. It was almost like the meetings, conversations and interviews never happened. With that said, there was still immense value in the experience for me. I may not have been 'Earvin's Guy' but I was worthy of the consideration, which gave me enormous confidence. Losses on big stages or at big moments means that you are close to something big and you are on the right path. After a disappointment, do not go into a 'tank'. Assess your strengths, skills, talents and go again. In considering Magic Johnson Enterprises' quest to monetize the urban market, the management staff I met with and some of the business deals, I felt very good about my chances to win in the urban market space too. This experience fueled my fire even more as I was destined to go 'all in' on creating a unique opportunity independent of Nike.

Another person that was aware of my pursuit of something greater was my friend Cynthia. She was the marketing lead for Fatburger. Cynthia was in the trenches of marketing to an ever-changing demographic similar to me. She also felt my same struggles, attempting to get upper management to get on board with the hip hop revolution happening right before our eyes. Cynthia suggested that I connect with Carl, my counterpart at Reebok. I had known of Carl just like I knew of John at Adidas and Pete at Fila. I made it my business to know my competitors. I met with Carl and we hit it off immediately. I felt his pain and he felt mine. He was experiencing upper management pushback to some of his innovative ideas to move the needle. To a degree, I was relieved. I must admit, despite Reebok's limitations, Carl was a formidable adversary in the LA footwear game. We both agreed we needed to make a move together and form an agency. Soon after, as fate would have it, I was returning from a vacation when first thing Monday morning a co-worker shuffled me into an office where I heard management from another group talking about me joining their group. That was not all. The reason I was up for discussion of joining the group was because of a company wide reorganization. When they moved on to another meeting topic, I went home to strategize. Conversations ensued about the re-org with my group. Fortunately, I had two opportunities. It was a tough time at Nike due to 'back door' human resources politics, people in the balance of being laid off and just the uncertainty of the future of the company. In addition to the two internal opportunities, I had landed another external offer to run sports marketing and programming for a media cable company. As I recollect, that offer was far better than both Nike offers but I was intrigued by one manager's offer. That intrigue quickly dissipated as the position was a national job managing twice the staff and was a lateral move in position and pay. The kicker was the explanation. The manager was trying to gently transition another worker out of his group due to embezzlement. And, to put it gently it was some of the same ole system, ism and privilege bullcrap. Damn, not again! But this made me think of how over the years this was in play at Nike even within my group.

    I had three managers in four years, and if I would have stayed at Nike it would have been four managers going into my fifth year. I was receiving pay increases and bonuses but no promotion opportunities. With every organizational change, I was never provided an opportunity to compete for a higher grade job but others seemed to land in the leadership positions within my organization. In New York, my guy Lincoln got railroaded out of the company when he bumped heads with a new manager. The narrative of his exit was centered on weak performance. When the manager handpicked Lincoln's replacement, the manager ended up shredding the guy he handpicked. Coincidentally, Lincoln and the handpicked guy were Black. Most of the managers directing and leading marketing in major metropolitan cities, where the key drivers for brand success was knowing the marketplace and having a superior understanding of urban culture, did not look like me. At the time, I looked at the game in play in Chicago and Atlanta as well as at Nike World Headquarters and advancement did not look promising. Lastly, during my run at Nike there were a substantial amount of Black men on the sales side. They were vital to growing urban accounts, providing the footwear designers feedback from athletes and teens and servicing retail businesses primarily to train retail workers on the superiority of Nike products. I interacted with those guys frequently nationwide as we had built a rapport and network. Continuously, there was no promise of advancement on that side of the business either.

As I looked at all of these scenarios with a critical eye and common sense, I decided that I would be better off leaving Nike and starting from scratch. If I was not provided one single opportunity of advancement in four years, I probably was not one of the 'chosen ones' and would probably just aimlessly drift within the company. As for the external sports marketing and programming job, I accepted it and then declined it. After my back to back experiences with great jobs at Chevron and Nike but no great opportunities for upward mobility, I figured I would give entrepreneurship a go.

Take a Leap of Faith: Go the Entrepreneur Route

At every major transition in my life, I knew what was in store for me. Matriculating through schools, I knew my next steps. Although I left Occidental College and Chevron, I knew where I was headed. But when I left Nike, I did not know what was coming next. I did not set up my business through my role at Nike. I did not fund another business through my role at Nike to step into an executive position with that company. And, I did not secure a major account for my new agency while at Nike. In essence, I was simply out there on a leap of faith. Up until this point, my dad never questioned any of my moves past the age of eighteen. We had a man-to-man talk about my professional journey up to that point. He understood the struggles, but did not understand me walking away from a relatively high-paying job to start a business. My pops had two employers most of his adult life, Uncle Sam and the County of Los Angeles. My mom had two employers most of her adult life, a hospital and the City of Los Angeles. My sister has had one employer most of her adult life, The County of Los Angeles. My brother Eric had multiple jobs but as of today, he's had one employer for the last 25 years, The Tribune Media Company. All of his adult life, my brother Alvin has never held a job or created his own lifestyle. My brother Fatty, well he was an untraditional entrepreneur in the realm of 'street commerce'. In short, this was a totally foreign concept to my dad, family and most of the people that I knew... even my Berkeley and Michigan comrades. At the end of the conversation, it was nothing but love and support from my dad but he did question my decision...and for a split second I did too. Good, bad, right or wrong, I was headed into the deep end of the pool and not knowing how deep the pool was.

Carl and I formed Urban Marketing Corporation of America (UMCA) and immediately hit the streets 'dialing for dollars'. Between the work both of us did in LA and for our respective companies, we were able to get meetings and serious consideration to run campaigns, provide marketing consulting and executive media buys. We did fairly well winning business from movie studios and cable networks that were striving to attract urban audiences and developing shows and movies starring Black characters. For instance, UMCA worked on nine Tyler Perry movies for Lionsgate. At the time, the Lionsgate staff simply did not know who Tyler Perry was in the streets and did not know how to market him or position his advertising and promotional campaigns. That's where we stepped in. We were also able to stay close to sports as my good friend George gave me a leadership position with the Michael Jordan Flight School in Santa Barbara, CA and Las Vegas, NV as well as the Vince Carter Basketball Camp in Barcelona. My former Nike hiring manager Jon had established an agency in Atlanta and awarded UMCA a few projects with Adidas working on

Kobe Bryant campaigns. Since I decided to depart from Nike as an employee, there was a reluctance to award business to UMCA. It served me well as I was able to 'plug in' to other brands, work styles, resources and marketing professionals to strengthen my breadth of knowledge and capabilities. It seemed like we had a few perfect storms every few months that afforded us unique opportunities and monies to expand our business.

Before long, The U was hummin'! We had a string of strategic partners that enabled us to get any job done. Our previous experiences allowed us to be masterful at building account teams, staying on task with projects and maintaining the integrity of budgets while sustaining a healthy profitable margin. The game changer for us came when we purchased The UMCA Global Compound as our corporate office. Not only were we a prominent Black-owned agency in Los Angeles with touchpoints to New York, Chicago and Atlanta, but it allowed us to serve as a gathering spot for an array of freelancers, creatives, entrepreneurs, thinkers, music and film producers and anyone striving to make their own way in business. Many people who gravitated to The U understood that our community possessed the DNA and blueprint to tap into what was happening in sports, entertainment, the arts, consumer products, etc. We all wanted to 'storm the castles', make some money and advance the culture. We were building something special, more than I had imagined.

Being the Lead with Nike Again

Another turning point came after a business trip from New York. I had just completed a project for HBO and made it home midday on a Monday. Carl was waiting outside my house. He shared that he had received a call from the Nike LA office and they wanted to meet immediately. It had been a couple of years since I had done any significant work with Nike. I was surprised, curious and energized by the proposition of getting back into the mix of The Swoosh. We met with the basketball lead, Jason. He and I went back to our time working at the Olympics and we worked on a few projects during my western region days at Nike. I would consider Jason a G.O.A.T of consumer experience and demand creation. I cannot say I know anyone who has done it better than him, including myself. Jason shared that he was tasked to successfully duplicate a program that management thought had great potential but fell flat when it was executed on the east coast. Jason described the program and his thoughts on elevating it in LA. Jason was on fire with ideas, but actually he stays on fire with ideas.

We took his thoughts back to the UMCA Global Compound, gathered our best thinkers and went to work on a pitch to send back to Jason and his team. He was feeling our direction and we went to work quickly building our budget, design execution, advertising, retail plan, etc. It was fairly easy for me to pick up the ball and run with it. I knew the Nike system and I had a few aces up my sleeve as well. Plus, my project team was phenomenal. All the major partners and friends of The U were vested in making the project a landslide winner. Since the project fell flat back east, there was a mass exodus from Nike WHQ that ascended on LA to experience our activation elements. I was confident as Jason served as a great leader taking care of the internal hurdles. We had support from Nike's North America basketball and brand design directors Todd and Ray respectively. At the time, Todd and Ray were the magic of Nike Basketball. The U was aligned strategically and tactically across all functions within Nike. Now all we had to do was, well 'Just Do It'. From the corporate and local 'check downs' to the retail and street team activations, to the look and feel of the space, to the product placement to the consumer experience, everything was off the charts. The joint was hot! Well, except for our musical entertainment, Snoop Dogg, blurting out a few expletive words to teens when our host location stated that there would be no profanity. Other than that, we were all good.

One of the things I loved about Jason was his competitive spirit with himself, his colleagues, serving consumers and athletes as well as his overall professional excellence. After our recent success, we embarked upon another landmark exploration of merging basketball, music, culture and all things hip hop. The project was formerly labeled as inauthentic in the Nike realm and it was unthinkable to consider the old school Nike regime. Honestly, the direction of the programming was everything me, Thaddeus and Jerry had crafted years ago with Represent. It was called Battlegrounds and it was a one-on-one tournament. I was no stranger to the Battleground concept because a year prior it was an apparel play built around a head-to-toe shoe, shirt and hat hook up that celebrated the hallowed grounds of city basketball. I helped my boy Mike at Nike connect some dots on the ground in LA to bring some hoop courts to fruition for the campaign. Timing is everything. I am glad I was still around to take advantage of the chance to be involved with what I started. Jerry was too, but Thaddeus had moved on from Nike.

Battlegrounds was designed to launch in New York and Los Angeles. Jason made the UMCA mission clear: be better than New York...period. I had a bit of a conflict because my good friend Gerry who introduced me to Nike was Jason's counterpart in New York. But there is nothing like a friendly East vs West rivalry. Plus, I was riding with Jason on this one because after a couple of years of me being 'left for dead' in the Nike world, Jason dusted me off and brought me back to life. Oddly enough, the LA Battlegrounds Championship was scheduled to be before New York's championship event. Although, when it came to basketball, New York was a self-proclaimed leader. In this case, they would follow figuratively and literally. Once again, for the LA Battlegrounds Championship, all Nike eyes were on LA, including the New York eyes and its Battlegrounds execution agency. We killed it! But we killed it from a strategic point of view in that it was no contest before things even started. We essentially put basketball in the middle of a night club, music video, happy hour, World Wrestling

Entertainment (WWE) type environment and Nike had never seen this possibility of sports and culture clashing with influencers, ballers and the like experiencing everything they loved in one place. A week later, I attended New York's championship event out of curiosity. I did not even stay until the end. Out of pure respect to my guy Gerry, I will just say that the LA Battlegrounds Championship was slightly better than New York's. From that point on, The U became the lead agency on all things Battlegrounds and Nike Basketball. And, my guy Jason? He was crowned 'King of the Court' by his colleagues.

Nike was UMCA's most high-profile client considering the large scale campaigns, sports positioning, iconic athletes and simply the brand cachet it carried in the marketing and advertising world. However, we had other great clients and supporters. During our heyday, The U did work year in and year out for the family of Time Warner, Viacom, Pepsi and Coca Cola companies. We had retainer agreements with HBO, Frito Lay, Pepsi North America, Nickelodeon and Cartoon Network to name a few. At some point, we changed our business name to UMCA Sports & Entertainment. Carl did an excellent job of cultivating and managing our entertainment business and I focused on our portfolio of sports relationships. He was able to parlay a Lionsgate relationship whereby we had a hand in the marketing mix of Tyler Perry's first 7 or 8 movies with Lionsgate. I still remember the marketing lead asking us during a meeting on another project, "Hey, have you heard of this Tyler Perry guy? I think he does church stage plays. We signed a deal with him, so I will probably need your help." Another great client was Nickelodeon. They were struggling to develop a strategy to capture boy segments and utilize urban marketing to be more than a suburban girl brand and network. Carl led the charge to work directly with the President and CMO to provide real, unfiltered insights and suggestions which led to significant paradigm shifts within the thinking of upper management. The U addressed the blind spots in the marketing plans for Lil Romeo's show to please his dad Master P. The ratings increased and the show became

Nickelodeon's #1 show for years. We were also brought in to work with Spike Lee's production company as Nickelodeon ventured to air its first Black live action mini-series. The content was powerful and we were tasked to work with Spike, his wife, the talent and Nickelodeon management to find a 'happy place' in terms of marketing, messaging, advertising and positioning. The mini-series did well for the first of its kind and inspired more content of that sort by the network. Nickelodeon's tent pole property was the Kids' Choice Awards. The management was using old thinking in terms of entertainment, lightweight guests and was not on the cusp of what was happening in youth culture with respect to cool, current trends and, of course, hip hop. Carl, the consummate smooth talker, was able to tactfully and eloquently communicate the need for vast and immediate changes, at least to the marketing of Kids' Choice Awards in order to attract more eyeballs, which translates to ratings.

Statistics conveyed that where The U was heavily involved in the creative, marketing and advertising process, there were clear and undeniable wins. We also transitioned from Nickelodeon to work for Cartoon Network when a high ranking executive made the jump. We had a history with the executive with another Viacom network as we worked on VH1 Hip Hop Honors to hike up its ratings. At Cartoon Network, we were right there for the development of its tent pole sports program 'Hall of Game' and stuck our nose in the early years of Adult Swim. Our most notable entertainment client by far was HBO. The cable network powerhouse was ahead of its time. Def Comedy Jam was epic in the world of Black culture. We were there for its return as well as the launch of Def Poetry. HBO gave us the keys to many of its sponsorship packages to create value, most notably the Essence Music Festival for 5 to 6 years. Its fearless leader at the time, Maria, was one of the most dynamic, passionate and brilliant individuals I have ever worked with. Gritty, sharp, quick and a go-getter, she pushed the limits of marketing to make cable affiliates nationwide enamored with HBO as more and more viewers flocked to each award-winning show. Over the years, viewership and affiliate relationships constantly grew under her watch.

It was great to be in the room to be a part of the strategy meetings and then being given marching orders to create campaigns and experiences to match the brand prominence and on air programming excellence. The U truly had the 'one-two punch' of sports and entertainment working to perfection.

In addition to our entertainment clientele growing, our national presence grew as well. After the LA Battlegrounds, Jason was elevated and tasked to lead a Battlegrounds Tour in 5 to 6 major markets throughout the USA. The U machine was right there lock and step to create magic and amazement in every market. We also worked more closely with Nike North America as the Battlegrounds Tour was the first of its kind in any sports category. The project allowed us to connect with leading artists, talent, hoopers, entertainers and local legends in each market to create relevant content. Nike and MTV2 teamed up to create a docu-mini series of Battlegrounds. This brought out the 'heavy artillery' to solidify its success. The G.O.A.Ts of brand design, Ray and Jimmy, held down advertising. My guy Gerry was running point on east coast markets and one of the unsung talents ever in the footwear game, Drew, led Nike west coast initiatives. We took the best of all thinking and built an epic movement in basketball, street and hip hop culture. In subsequent years, Battlegrounds went global and even included NBA Players. Nike Basketball and MTV2 won. We smashed it. More importantly, The U leveraged our strategies and techniques to manage tours for the Jordan Brand, HBO, Pepsi, Nickelodeon and Cartoon Network. And, having 'boots on the ground' soldiers in key markets, we were able to offer nationwide promotional campaigns and programming for our entertainment clients that wanted to touch, move and inspire the urban communities around movie premiers and television series. I did not know what the future would hold day-to-day, but this was truly an exciting time that had me eager to face each day with optimism, joy and aspiration.

Building the Right Team

I would be remiss not to share that nothing great is done alone. UMCA was not built merely by Carl and me. The U had an extraordinary collection of young talent, creatives, intellects and geniuses that embraced our vision and delivered best in class work product over and over. In our early years, two people stand out as unique individuals that elevated our brand and bolstered our business. Knowing the streets, hip hop trends and having tentacles to those worlds was vital. Our guy David got us there at light speed and kept us there. He ran all of our street team activations, sampling programs and promotion campaigns. He also worked with numerous record labels and hip hop brands enabling us to create partnerships, co-branding campaigns and he commingled our projects with top rappers and R&B artists. He is a brilliant brotha. Before digital became what it is today, Cyndee made us innovative leaders in our field. Through the use of emails, newsletters, pop-up web pages and the latest digital techniques, we were able to enhance our marketing and advertising offerings as well as go deeper with corporate brands by tapping into its emerging digital groups and its advertising departments. Cyndee went on to develop proprietary content delivery software for a movie studio. We were lucky to catch her before she and her company blew up.

Our next round of game changing talent was centered around the need to communicate and articulate our work, ideas and the urban landscape. Many key decision makers, gatekeepers and budget approvers were people that did not understand the urban market, hip hop, or how Black people ignited trends and what was going on outside of the ivory towers. The cornerstone of UMCA videos, recaps and presentations helped us to bridge the gap on understanding, learning and, most of all, justifying hiring UMCA. We utilized three talented people. The first was my creative director, Daven. I connected Daven with our client's creative lead to obtain brand style guides and to be current with what works for companies from a look and feel perspective. Daven worked with numerous movie studios and local businesses, he was dialed in. The second was Diann, who later became my wife. She was a photographer so I was able to get images for all the UMCA work. I would team her up with Daven and David's teams to produce killer visual presentations that told the story. Lastly, was my big brother, Eric. He was a cameraman for a local news station. He knew how to produce and shoot long and short segments. Plus, he knew character generation and editing. He was a sports and entertainment fan and had flavor. I probably still owe him money from all of the overnight editing sessions. Our final ascent from a talent perspective came when we began to do large scale productions, build out spaces and produce projects outside of Los Angeles. We truly had to step up our game to serve a number of clients. My first move was to get a superstar designer and producer that understood urban life. We landed Diann who had built a career making raw spaces opulently magnificent. She became our go-to producer and brought an army of creative talent and vendors to UMCA. Her nickname became Spitfire. She was the first and last 'Queen B' of The U. The final piece of the puzzle was our production lead. We grabbed Mark who had a history of set designing some of the most notable hip hop music videos by multi-platinum artists. He saw possibilities that I could not see in a million years when it came to erecting greatness on concrete, dirt or walls. Sorry, I cannot stop there with the shout outs. I must give praise to Remy and Robyn who were Carl's right hands holding down entertainment. Ebony and Anna who were my right hands on sports. Paul who was all things operations. Drego was all things East Coast; UF who led athlete camps and elite youth basketball programs and my former Nike colleague Lincoln who was my road warrior leading tours and out of state programming. As time passed, we had waves of new talent that also did their thing with

The U. As I think about it, I could go on and on about other team members, partners and vendors that contributed mightily to UMCA that resided in Los Angeles, Chicago, New York, Atlanta, Washington DC and San Francisco. I celebrate them all as I saw and continue to see their careers and businesses flourish. The U was like a great recipe, every ingredient counted and made the meal stupendous. I am forever grateful and a better person because of the love, effort, commitment and excellence delivered by this marvelous collection of people from all walks of life.

The Emergence of Multicultural Marketing

As great as our growth was, it did not come without struggle. As the world became more enamored with hip hop, creating new types of icons and leveraging street culture, it meant that the face of marketing and advertising changed significantly. The face of the power structure and ultimate decision makers did not change per se, but the faces up and down the infrastructure of organizations changed. In addition, urban marketing quickly became multicultural marketing. And, when you consider this shift along with more people thinking and wanting to convey knowledge of the urban space and interjecting opinions, points of views and the like, things become super competitive, bland and unjust in more ways than one. Leadership and management in Corporate America were laggards in discovering how influential and profitable the urban space had become. The systems and businesses that support Corporate America which also lagged, quickly caught on to the movement. Our biggest forms of competition became internal employees wanting to create opportunities for themselves given the flow of dollars that were heading away from traditional marketing to this influx of interest in urban and multicultural marketing. We began to take heed that movie studio marketing managers were forming their own agencies and acquiring business from their friends within the industry. We also saw this happening at consumer product goods companies. At HBO, we had a good run, but our last project was based on a Latino talent driven mini-series. We placed our Latino marketing guy Luis on the job. There were some questionable decisions regarding strategy in one of the markets. Our suggestions were not implemented and the program fell short. A few days later, we participated in a meeting to discuss the shortcomings. We were rolled off of the project and a multicultural agency backed by a HBO general market agency was in place. The movement to general market agencies handling multicultural agencies was in full effect. Hey, all is fair in business and power. The shocker for me was what I saw happening at Nike on a regional and national level. The U was involved in preliminary conversations to do a huge project in LA. Based on my history in LA and our previous wins for Nike across the country, my internal contact and I thought it was a foregone conclusion that UMCA would be working on the project.

This would be the biggest project the regional office had ever embarked on. Soon after receiving the quick briefing, I was called by the Nike management who had just left a project planning meeting and wanted to meet with me personally. I was told that UMCA would not be part of the project. The meeting felt like my Chevron exit meeting with Marty. There was an apologetic tone and a remorseful manner in the conversation. This individual was new to the company and had power but would not wield it. I did not like or appreciate it, but I got it. The only thing I took exception to was that Nike cobbled together a collection of vendors that executed the program poorly. The team lead also tried to use many of the people that The U had trained and used in the past but excellence was generated by cobbling those pieces as well. The formula was off. The recipe was missing something. In the end, I was informed by an array of Nike management in Beaverton and Los Angeles that the program did not meet up to its expectations. Nevertheless, UMCA never worked on a Nike project after that. Also, the consensus was that it was a 'money grab and strategic play' to shift the power dynamics and cash flow of marketing budgets into different pockets. A few years later, a similar scenario also occurred with Nike on the national level. Pursuant to a successful national, first ever domestic national tour with LeBron James followed by managing Nike's presence at The Dream Team Naismith Hall of Fame Induction, The U was essentially displaced by a general market agency. Fortunately, the money grab and clandestine relationship with the general market agency was laid out to me by a few high-ranking Nike executives. So many knew the play...and the game. This was well played because these Nike cases, like some of the others with our entertainment and consumer product goods clients, are still benefiting after all these years from the culture and 'white glove' access into business fortune. I thought I was done with school after Michigan. This learning right here was a system, ism and privilege lesson of the highest order. I could not believe it. I saw it happening again and I still did not believe it; but I believe it now.

After building a business from scratch, seven consecutive years of producing national tours, numerous theatrical release campaigns, cable network launches, athlete programming, NBA All Star weekend activations, serving sports and entertainment brands, working with athletes and being 'all in' with clients, staff and projects, I decided to divest from UMCA. I simply had to rethink a lot of things. I had hit a wall one April around a Final Four project. My joy, excitement and focus simply was not there. I noticed the changing landscape of who UMCA was truly serving, our role within projects and the treatment of us versus other agencies. The leadership of corporate marketing changed. I was not going into battle to do groundbreaking projects with the Jasons, Marias, Drews and Rays of the world any more. UMCA probably could have used a capital infusion so that I could have hired 2 to 3 more senior people to fulfill certain roles to insulate me from these realities, but we did not get that done. Carl and I had received two offers to purchase UMCA. One offer was from a Canadian company that wanted The U to transform into its west coast office. Neither Carl or I were wild about the employment agreement we would have had to commit to. Another offer came from a theatrical brand design and marketing entity. We could not make the numbers and ownership percentage work. Kobe Bryant and I had a conversation about him buying UMCA but he snapped up some advertising guys to form a traditional ad agency.

The biggest reason I divested was because I truly needed a break and I could not obtain one if I was still connected to The U. I was too much of 'it' from a client, strategy and execution standpoint. Good, bad, right or wrong, I felt I was in too deep to reinvent myself. I can kick myself by thinking that my continuous work, travel and living a 'good life' took the place of long vacations, sabbaticals or self reflection. If I had realized this, I may have conjured up ways to pivot, reimagine and lead The U until I died because I truly found a great rhythm. But such is life. Plus, moving through Chevron, Nike and working with Corporate America was taxing. UMCA earned every dime and penny we made. We were never at ease from our first payment to the last I benefited from. We won for our clients or we were shown the door. I was not sure that place was where my heart was even though I owned 50% and it was even more of who I was. How did it actually end? Carl and I had drinks on the Venice Beach Boardwalk reminiscing about the great ride of UMCA. We shared tons of laughs, learnings and fond recollections. As we toasted our marvelous journey together, Carl took the UMCA baton and kept running the company like the anchor leg of a relay race. Me, I graciously handed him the baton, slowed down and gathered myself like the third leg of a relay race routinely does. The U for me was no more. Great times. I have nothing but love for Carl. That brotha gave me the best opportunity I ever had in my life up to that point.

Key Takeaways

- If powerful, influential people provide you with an audience, take full advantage of it. Mesmerize them with your intellect, talents and gifts. More importantly, engage them in a manner where you stand to learn from them as well.

- Take chances on yourself and find others who are risk takers. Risk takers are the people who change the world. Be one of those people. Jobs are cool but adventures are better.

- Build a team and a system that is built to last. Secure the most talented and creative people to lead your charge. Always do groundbreaking work and don't settle for less.

8

Mr. International

> *A man who is not courageous enough to take risks will never accomplish anything in life.*
>
> MUHAMMED ALI

When I was a youth, I rarely traveled. Other than driving to Pomona, which is just outside of Los Angeles, to visit my grandmother, Aunt Barbara and cousins, I was pretty much in and around my neighborhood. There was also the occasional Vegas run with my parents, but no trains or planes. When I was a teen, I branched out a little bit. My bike became the primary conduit for exploring new worlds. However, the numerous gang territories within my neighborhood limited my range of travel. I had a car at sixteen and that expanded my exploration even further, but it too had its 'limitations'. Even though I lived in an environment riddled with gang activity, my parents were more concerned and cautious of the police when I left my house by car. Not due to the possibility of getting a traffic violation, but the distinct likelihood of being harassed, beaten or killed by the police...the typical bullcrap we still hear about frequently wherever Black people live in the USA. My house was located in an area controlled by the 77th Precinct of the Los Angeles Police Department. If you Google this precinct, you will discover many were tyrants, drug dealers, thieves, thugs and actually the most notorious gang in LA at the time. Between the gangs, police and isms from typical residents of Southern California, I tended to stay close to my home and hood. With respect to my parents, I can only recall my mom being on a plane twice, once to attend her dad's funeral and the other to see family in Oklahoma and Missouri. As for my dad, I only recall him being on a plane once and that was when he attended my Michigan MBA graduation. In essence, we were a sedentary family.

When I was a student at Cal, I stayed on a similar course–my travel habits remained the same. Other than heading back to LA from time to time, I did not venture too far from my new home in the Bay Area, other than Tahoe and Reno runs in hopes of gambling to pay rent or tuition. Of course, at Cal there were diverse students from varied socio-economic backgrounds so I heard numerous travel stories; from extravagant summer vacations to 'girls gone wild' spring break stories to impromptu Mexico and Hawaii trips. I could only visualize and speculate what those experiences were like; I was never jealous or envious, per se, but highly interested. As for many of the upwardly mobile Black students, the most talked about getaway from Cal and the Bay Area was to travel to Howard University's Homecoming Weekend in Washington, DC. I was even more intrigued by this idea, but it was in the middle of the semester. I simply could not afford being away from work or take on the expense of the trip. Unknowingly, I was being bottled up in Los Angeles as well as in the Bay Area through my youth, teens and early adulthood. I believe it was predestined that I would accept the job at Occidental College where I could stretch out a bit. It was a sign of more travel opportunities to come.

Throughout my Occidental College, Nike and UMCA career days, I had traveled quite a bit throughout the USA. I was a regular in cities such as New York, San Francisco, Chicago, Atlanta, Washington, D.C., Portland, Las Vegas, Dallas and Detroit. It was not until I worked with my guy George that I began to really travel. George, who is a G.O.A.T. in global basketball, is also a member of the Naismith Basketball Hall of Fame. I previously worked with George on the Michael Jordan Basketball Camp project for many years. He was also tasked to produce a camp in Barcelona for NBA legend and future Hall of Fame member Vince Carter, also known as Vinsanity. Vince was on fire as a player and he was a major basketball icon at the time. The goal was to extend that heat to Europe.

Years prior, the USA Basketball Dream Team had paved the way in the Olympics, so Vinsanity was just keeping the fire lit. The experience was mind-blowing! I had been accustomed to the finer elements of travel, but rolling with basketball royalty like Vince and George was a whole other level entirely. The five-star hotels, fine dining and red carpet treatment opened my eyes to a different world. In Barcelona, we had the 'hostess with the mostess' in my man Rich. He was a Nike consultant but resided in all parts of Europe. Rich was smooth, savvy, worldly and genuinely a nice guy. I watched his every move and how he operated. I could not wait until the day was over for him to show us adventure after adventure in Barca. And, the work was cool too. George kind of gave me the keys to the project as I was the youngin' of the crew. I enjoyed taking the baton and running with it. Also, Vince had a number of Nike responsibilities that I took the lead on as well. I was the American so the Barcelonians probably figured I was his manager. Little did they know, the Black woman in the wings was calling the shots...Vince's mom. Everywhere we went it was bananas! Shout out to Vince, he was all in on the cultural aspects of Barcelona which meant that we covered a lot of ground in the city. For Vince, it was about more than basketball as we were educated on art, religion, people, history, culture, food and all things Barcelona and in the surrounding regions within Europe. Vince helped lay the groundwork for how I would attack international travel for the rest of my life.

After Barcelona, I sought out more experiences outside of the USA. As hip hop matured, there was a movement to be 'ghetto fabulous'...poppin' bottles, buying out the bar, fast cars, jewelry, designer clothes, etc. I loved hip hop music and culture but I was never into the acquisition of the "stuff" as a youth and definitely not as an adult. I cherished rich experiences and being in the midst of uniqueness, different environments and new adventures. And that is why I love my wife, Diann. She was and still is a travel fiend. She loves the multiple benefits of travel as well as all the brands the rappers were singing about. The difference between my wife and the rappers was she would not run down to the mall or Rodeo Drive to buy expensive items. Her thing was going to the actual fashion houses in Europe, meeting with the design director then purchasing with an understanding and appreciation of the fabrics, leathers, craftsmanship, stories and meanings. All of that was cool, but it all was still overpriced for me! Through wifey's role as a luxury lifestyle event planner and designer, we were able to travel extensively throughout Central America and Europe for both business and pleasure. I became infatuated with the international lifestyle, meeting different types of people, learning about various cultures and most of all, experiencing an entirely new vibe.

Meeting Any Challenge: The Beginning of an Incredible Journey

On the tail end of UMCA, I had moved to Atlanta to take the lead on our Turner Broadcasting/Cartoon Network deal. One day while in Atlanta, I received a call from my Nike guy, Brandon. He was moving up the ranks at Nike and he had moved to Shanghai to lead Nike Greater China Basketball. He was heading up a huge countrywide multi-faceted project in Shanghai that would be the biggest campaign that Nike Greater China (Nike GC) had ever embarked upon. He articulated the enormous challenge of blue-skying the strategy and developing the game plan for the entire team. His job was to take the vision's possibility and desired outcomes and turn it into a reality. Of course, on the other side of every challenge is an opportunity. Brandon hit my sweet spot by taking me down memory lane and inviting me to join him on this new path. To say the least, I was sold. He did share one hurdle, I had to obtain approval from the #1 marketing executive at Nike GC. He offered me a trip to Beijing to be part of the project kick off, meet the team and impress his boss. That was all he promised...and that was all I needed. I arrived in Beijing and my body clock was off. To energize myself, I decided to get a quick workout in before the kickoff meeting. There was one other guy in the hotel gym. I hopped on the treadmill beside him. This dude was rolling at an incredible pace. All I kept thinking about was Will Smith's claim that when it comes to hard work, and if you place him side by side with another person on a treadmill, he would outlast that person or die. Well, I was already dying trying to keep up with this guy so I decided to outlast him. The minute he calmly completed his workout, I died on the side of my treadmill. We exchanged light banter before he left. When I arrived at the meeting, I did not know anyone but Brandon. We caught up quickly then he took his seat in the front of the meeting room. The room was packed. People were sneaking looks at me...and me sneaking looks at them. Then, the head guy took his place in the front of the room to start the meeting. It was the guy from the gym! At the break, I made my way to meet Simon, who was the fearless marketing leader at Nike GC. We had a good laugh about the gym scenario. During the series of kickoff meetings, I jumped in where I saw I could offer some value. The ideation was pretty awesome and aggressive. I was feeling it. At the final team dinner, Brandon strategically sat me next to Simon. By the end of the dinner, Simon gave the green light for me to become a part of the team. This moment would mark the beginning of an incredible journey.

When I arrived in Shanghai, I had no idea what I was about to encounter moving forward. New country, language, culture, rituals, lifestyle and a totally different relationship with sports than in the USA. Brandon had been an 'old pro' at living a normal life in Greater China. He did everything he could to acclimate me but it was up to me to take on integrating into the team, grasping the culture, working the plan, making friends and allies, creating confidence and all personal matters. I jumped right in. I began to meet one-on-one with all entities internally and externally associated with the campaign including Nike GC's slate of agencies. I studied the Nike GC business initiatives, category marketing plans, advertising and media partnerships, digital strategy and sports marketing positioning. Everything was fair game and could be leveraged against this campaign. I was able to travel to Beijing, Hong Kong and Taiwan to learn its marketplace and get a better feel for the landscape. Friendships began to form, trust was building, ingenious ideas sprung out of nowhere and the team's vision was beginning to take shape and form. We got to a good place relatively quick and I was all in.

The work rhythm was cool, but I began to feel like something was still missing. Monday 9am through Friday at 2pm was a breeze for me. The tough time came during the summer months when the office closed after 2pm on Friday. At times I would wake up on Saturday, workout twice, eat two meals, read two books, watch two movies and it would only be 11am. Not true of course, but the weekends felt so slow until I found my stride. I found an array of great Chinese restaurants, a burger joint, a Mexican restaurant, a pizza spot and a local market. Also, I found self-care...something I had never tried before. The price point on massages and manicures were such that I had one of each every week. I usually do not admit this, but I have had a bad nail biting and skin picking obsessive control disorder for as long as I can remember. I just can't help myself as I subconsciously do this all the time. I stopped biting my nails when I had them done every week. Unfortunately, I am only a non-nail biter in Shanghai. There was a Europeanized area of the city called the French Concession. It was cool hanging out there as well. I found a pastry shop that I would run to every Sunday morning. They would make a custom croissant with eggs and cheese for me. After my meal, I would watch the people do Tai Chi in a nearby park then run back to my hotel.

I also got my 'sexy on' while I was in Shanghai. I lost about 30 pounds working out everyday, spending time in the steam room, sauna and pool. Also, I didn't have a heavy diet of processed food there. Of course, as I developed friendships I would meet people for meals, drinks, etc. The only thing missing was having my wife with me.

As for the project itself with Nike GC, I had reached another mountaintop. I cannot begin to share how personally gratifying this project was. The Nike GC team was a group of relatively young professionals new to the workplace as well as to Nike. Our team was literally creating Nike in China and its history along the way. The Nike GC team was outstanding. I had seen an organization genuinely come together, grow confidence, pride and become fearless in the face of all the pressures we encountered. For instance, I will always remember when Brandon had to make a tough decision to trim the budget. It seemed like every night we would go over the budget. From a budgetary standpoint, his butt was on the line with Simon. Simon was cool, but he was not that cool about blowing up a project budget. Brandon decided to trim my man Eric's Nike Sportswear budget. Eric was hot! Brandon and Eric had a great relationship, but not that night. I had never in my career witnessed a man with so much passion, conviction, commitment and determination fight so freakin' hard. To Eric, it was not about his budget, it was about his consumer, the movement within his category and delivering something Greater China had not seen before. I was blown away and truly moved. Brandon and Simon made sure Eric had everything he needed and he did his thing. His campaign, outreach and activation was phenomenal. He had the type of energy that was built and fueled by the Nike GC project overall. Simon was masterful in his leadership, coaching and driving each team member...including myself. Brandon was magnificent in his vision, driving the processes and demanding excellence. Each category leader was awesome, dynamic and unselfish. It was truly an honor to be a part of this team. The program was nominated for Nike's highest honor, but unfortunately it fell short of winning. We came back the following year and did it bigger and better. Once again, a phenomenal success. We were more successful than the year prior, but it was expected. The consensus within management was that we could not eclipse what the team had just done. After that year, it was a wrap. But I would not be done in China. I returned to do projects for a gaming company with clients including the NFL and NBA China and the beloved Kobe Bryant. I also returned to do a huge Jordan Brand project. I cannot lie, China was very good to me. My experience there helped me to grow in profound ways, culturally and as a human being, more than I could ever have imagined.

Imagining a Nike Brasil Brand: No Problem, No Fear

My wife and I were enjoying our anniversary in Paris where we were planning to get married again, I think for the third time. I was following her around, as she was probably shopping, when a weird number popped up on my phone. I answered. On the other line was Tim, the head of marketing for Nike Brasil, along with the head of events, Vini. The team in South America was embarking on the largest campaign the group had ever been tasked to perform. The office was ramping up and getting ready for the World Cup and the 2016 Olympics. This project was the igniter to demonstrate to the continent and to the world that Nike would be a leader in building up the country through sport. Tim and Vini wanted to know my interest level of being a part of the project. Hmmm...an experience in Brasil? I was sold the moment I heard Brasil. The rest was just blah, blah, blah. But for real, I was lucky to be in the midst of renewing my vows in Paris because that is the only way I would have gotten permission to take an assignment anywhere near Brasil. Our renewal ceremony and Paris was incredible to say the least. The Eiffel Tower, Fashion Houses and the incredible French food were amazing. In fact, we had so much fun, wifey took me to a strip club called the Crazy Horse. It is a joke...those who know, know.

Upon my return to LA, I packed and then I was off to São Paulo the next day. By now, I knew how to plug into a city so that was not too much of a problem. Plus, the culture in São Paulo was festive, friendly and outgoing. There was always something to do, the art and cultural scene was crazy. The hip hop vibes were everywhere. São Paulo seemed familiar. The only issue was language. Unlike China, a lot of people in Brasil outside the professional environment do not speak English, and I did not know Portuguese. My broken Spanish only got me so far. I was coached up by the GM of my hotel on how to handle myself around the neighborhood. He essentially told me not to wear my nice Nike product on the weekends while walking around. He brought me some local t-shirts from the mall a few blocks down the street to wear. He encouraged me to fit in and not to talk to anyone. He was clear...do not let people know that you are a foreigner. I took his words to heart. Unfortunately, a few months prior, some Nike executives were held up at gunpoint in their hotel. All accounts pointed to an inside job possibly. No problem. No fear. I listened, learned and did what the GM said. I kept my head on a swivel and kept to myself when I was alone.

In terms of the work, once again it was off the charts. A funny thing happened. When the management team was briefing me on the essence of what we were striving to create, build and achieve, Tim showed a video of Nike Battlegrounds and asked if I was familiar with it. My guy Ray in brand design was down there as well imagining a Nike Brasil Brand signature look and developing talent. We chuckled and Tim proceeded. It was a young, scrappy, passionate team that was striving to do the impossible. I loved the underdog hustle of the team and its quest to do the incredible and amazing. It is inspiring how sports galvanized pride, passion and the full extension of one's ability. The team was also multicultural, coming from various parts of the world and the South American continent. This added to the richness of the work, programming and experience. Henry, who was the #1 executive in Brasil, truly let the team do its thing.

I remember the project demands, timelines and pressure ascended at a boiling point. You could cut the tension with a knife. I proceeded to talk to Tim about it. We had a major briefing meeting with Henry the next day to share the team's progress to date. Tim called a mandatory happy hour meeting that evening. At about 1am, and yes I was drunk, but not too drunk to remind Tim we had a meeting in the morning with Henry. Tim called Henry on the spot! Henry simply moved the meeting to the afternoon. The content of the meeting did not change, but that happy hour brought the entire team together. Without question, Tim's decision was the best. I have never seen such a bold and gutsy leadership move that transformed the energy and spirit of our entire group. Even more impressive, Henry did not ask anything about the 1am call or the meeting reschedule until after the meeting was over. And it was not even a big issue when he learned of the reason. We went on to achieve unprecedented milestones, and I still hear that our achievements in Rio de Janeiro remain unmatched.

We put together a monster campaign in four markets within Brasil and we had a flawless unique event activation on the sands of Copacabana. We made Brasilians proud as we brought over 100,000 people to the beach to experience a united front of new faces in the form of athletes, entertainers and influencers coming together for one cause— the love of the national sport, futbol. I loved everything about this project and I thoroughly enjoyed my time in Brasil. I appreciated the culture, people and environment similar to my time in China. As for my return to the country, I was a 'one and done' in Brasil. Tim and Vini offered another shot at taming lightning in a bottle, but I had some conflicts. It was time to come home according to wifey.

DAMON HALEY

New Perspective: Being a Black Man in Another Country

My wife's agency also afforded us the opportunity to travel on business to places such as Moscow, Lagos, Cairo, Istanbul, Puerto Rico, Riviera Maya and Bahrain to name a few places. My all-time 'my wife is working and I am not' country is Italy. She shot a television show called, "To Rome for Love" for four months and I tagged along. For the first week, I was the supportive husband. After that, everyday I was like, "Let's catch up when you get off." I would take trains and buses to explore every direction outside of Rome. Plus, on her days off we would go to cities like Bologna, Florence, Naples, Venice and the Amalfi Coast. During my stint in Rome, I was able to work remotely on consulting projects.

A realization I discovered was generated by two men in particular. One was my Cuban-Roman brother, Alejandro. I have been all over the world working with a lot of people of different cultures. But, for the first time I was able to obtain a perspective about being a Black man in another country. And not from a Black American perspective, but an Afro-Cuban man being raised as an Afro-Italian. The conversations I had with Alejandro blew me away. He is a sharp, cultured, classy, smart guy. He is true to his bloodline. He is nurturing as a passionate Cuban and a debonaire Italian. Alejandro shared the experience of Blacks in Rome, Italy and Europe. As you may be aware, the geography of Europe and its countries is like state borders in the USA, they are extremely close. He broke it all down. Some of his points sounded eerily familiar and others were brand new to me. It was highly impactful to hear a young guy talking about our plight...not his, our plight as Black men navigating life all over the world. I thought I could escape the trappings of racism and privilege in a land far away from the USA, but that simply was not the full picture. The second guy, Lance Blanks. Lance is as American as they come. He is a Texas boy. I had toggled back and forth from Florida and Rome as I was working with Lance. When I initially told my wife about the Florida project she rejected it. She had the Italy master plan for our trip all drawn out. But, when I told her the project was supporting Lance, and he was the first and only Black CEO and high level executive to award me a job or consulting project, she said, "Go help your friend." Lance was the CEO of a sports business. Lance's political, social, economic sensibilities are off the charts. He truly would school me and share his insights, analysis and projections on people, issues and scenarios. One experience in particular with Lance that summer sticks out. We were heading into a meeting with the owner of the company, Mike. Lance grabs me and says, "D, you do not have to prove anything to Mike. Just tell him what we should be doing." After the meeting, we had an expansive discussion on his comment but the crystalized version was that Lance said I was his guy...period. I was there because I was the subject matter expert. I was highly accomplished. It's unfortunate that Black folks always feel we have to prove our position and worth. We feel so often that our voices aren't heard unless we overachieve and outperform in high-pressure environments. Do not fall into the trap. Lance hit me with some real grown Black man nuggets of truth during our magical time working together.

With Alejandro in one ear and Lance in the other in Florida, I had an 'ah ha' moment. My Greater China, Brasil and other business outside of the USA were void of the impact of systems, isms and privilege. Not once did they come up and turn things around. Outside the USA, I did not experience the funky stuff, the bullcrap during my 6 to 7 tours in Greater China or Brasil. I did not feel that the systems, isms and privilege clouds were raining on me and I had to protect myself with a raincoat or an umbrella. As I walked the streets, saw the police, interacted with people and dealt with city officials, business owners and agencies, I did not sense that being Black had anything to do with anything. I didn't even get any weird awkward insensitive probing questions about our racial, ethnic or physical differences. When talking about sports or hip hop, which the projects included, there was not a hint of race...only the athletic excellence, dope lyrics and hyped beats were referenced. Good, bad, right or wrong, I believe that in addition to having phenomenal teams and resources, I was able to produce exceptional results because I did not have to navigate with the 'raincoat' on and I did not have to use an 'umbrella'. And, oddly enough, the leadership on my international projects and business ventures were all non-Americans. All interesting and thought-provoking ideas, but despite the realizations I was not quite ready to relinquish my U.S. citizenship.

Key Takeaways

- Test your limits physically, geographically, mentally and culturally. Earth is a big place. You grow exponentially when you experience other cultures, places and ways of doing things. Don't just Google it. Go see it.

- In order to perform at a high level you must steady your mind. It is tough to do this with the systems, isms and privileges always at work. If you can block out the psychological noise at key moments when you need to rise up, you will have phenomenal success.

- Life is different for Black folks outside of the United States, it's worth experiencing different sides of yourself abroad. Trust me.

9

Nothing Lasts Forever

> *If you strike me down, I shall become more powerful than you can possibly imagine.*
>
> — OBI-WAN KENOBI, *STAR WARS*

Over two decades, I was able to be at the forefront of what turned out to be incredible global brands, icons, and movements. I truly believe that I used everything I had in terms of education, experience, talent, relationships, as well as creativity, innovation, management and leadership skills to produce an unprecedented curriculum vitae. From a range of projects with my UMCA clientele, my international consulting assignments, contributions to my wife's business and the people I have had the pleasure of working with along the way, I was truly blessed and highly favored. One would think that I would be invaluable to the marketing system and the business of sports for a lifetime but that was not the case for me. I truly do not know what it is, but I believe I lacked a vital element. I would give a king's ransom to have it deciphered for me. However, I currently characterize it as I do not possess the vital ingredients that it takes for my curriculum vitae recipe to be over the top. I did not have the one straw that would have broken the camel's back to abundantly award me something extraordinary within the sports industry. I felt all the signs were there too. I just never was able to acquire the GPS System to navigate to my sport's mountaintop.

DAMON HALEY

When The System Needs You & When It Doesn't

Carl cultivated the UMCA Entertainment business and holds the intimate knowledge of how the client relationships shifted and/or ended. The most professional and considerate 'dis' I have ever had from an individual and company was with Pam from Nickelodeon. She summoned Carl and me to meet with her on one of her visits to Los Angeles. She shared our wins and value to the Viacom family of networks, but notified us that our contract would not be renewed. We had real talk about the agency landscape and shifting C-Suite thoughts on marketing, advertising, the digital space, viewers, diversity and the business of content. She was a straight shooter. In a workman type fashion, we met for approximately one hour in a Chinese fast food restaurant one block from her Burbank studio. I never thought our Nickelodeon scenario would last forever because its marketing and viewer acquisition shifted, and there was a new leadership regime. We saw the writing on the wall, and fortunately we had received word from other Viacom managers about the topic of our meeting with Pam. Despite Pam wielding the guillotine that day, I was totally resolved as she left the table. Carl and I finished up lunch, had some 'oh well, it was good while it lasted' conversation and made our way back to LA. Clearly, our time was up with Nickelodeon.

Quiet as it's kept, in the sports world, women play a huge role in terms of the marketing function. Although men often hold the C-Suite and upper management roles, women have made incredible strides to climb the corporate ladder to make a huge impact in the sports industry, particularly in consumer product goods and retail service segments. Similar to my final experience with Pam, I had another tough executive deliver a rough, rugged and raw message to me. She is still in the marketing game, so she shall remain nameless. This executive and I posted some major wins together at Nike. On one occasion, she called me in distress and simply said, "Can you be here tomorrow because I have a problem." I quickly hopped on a plane and I was there. The project was interesting because it involved a world-class athlete, but more importantly, I was there for my colleague.

The mission was simple, make it right and we managed to do just that. One early morning, we both were working out in the gym of a hotel and we both were working on a major Nike project. I asked tough questions about my role and the overall feeling about me within the walls of Nike. She shared that there was a movement to phase me out of the picture. She identified two people that were the primary drivers of the movement, and how it was being done. With time as my witness, she was spot on...the tactics, verbiage, and the intricate details. The most surprising and helpful element of the discussion was that she urged me to find another way because, despite my previous successes, there was a silent consensus as others stood by and witnessed what was going on. She admitted it was unjust, but she helped me to read the tea leaves. And, she was sincere, caring, and insightful as she unveiled the harsh reality. She shared that in her opinion I was Nike's Rambo. I would only be summoned if a project was high stakes, as Nike management knew the other agencies that were being positioned and elevated had distinct limitations and capabilities. I was in utter disbelief. The game and power players were trying their hardest to keep me out of the playing field. They weren't neutral at all, in fact, it was completely biased.

All the while, I was in the middle of a multifaceted program that was high profile, involved numerous moving parts and produced winning results. I took heed of my dear friend's words. I respected her for sharing so candidly. I was elated at the heads up and decided to workout that morning. I had already been bumped out of Nike LA a few years back, so I had somewhat of a game plan for circumstances such as this. I was able to build business and acumen in other parts of the country. As she stated, invitations to work on projects went to zero with no real reasoning or communication. I was grateful though as that conversation opened up my treks to China and beyond. The conversation with my dear friend that morning revealed the end of my tenure with Nike North America...so I thought.

Playing Rambo for the Last Time

Fortunately, a few years later Nike North America was in need of a Rambo in a major metropolitan market that had lost ground to Adidas. A little cache with local influencers and one particular sports category needed more muscle with its tent pole local sports property. And, on the horizon, a major North American campaign and a global event was heading to that market. All eyes would be riveted on this campaign, marketplace elevation and event activation. 'Colonel Troutman' in the form of Nike management at world headquarters as well as the local marketing director felt that I would add immediate and significant value to the team. The mission as always...post a blowout victory. After five months of planning, strategizing, working across sports categories and functions, tireless nights and weekends, we were victorious. The project was awarded Nike's highest honor. I was even provided an opportunity as part of the project to travel to Barcelona with the marketing team. It felt good being back in the USA doing great work, and this project indirectly impacted lives significantly. To this day, I still receive calls from project partners, participants and vendors. Flash forward nine months, there is an opportunity to become one of that market's agency of record. I discussed the potential opportunity with the sports category marketing lead. We went back and forth discussing possibilities. I shared that I would move my family to that market to ensure the highest level of day-to-day service, thought partnering, strategy and execution. The result...the category selected a different agency of record. I thought for sure delivering Nike's highest honor would grant me the highest of consideration or at minimum an opportunity to fail, which is something that had never happened on a project I was associated with. I began to understand that there was a certain hypocrisy in meritocracy. Serious systems, isms and privilege were in play...and working diligently. The writing was on the wall that I was done in that market. And when I say done, I really mean done.

The following year, a Request for Proposal (RFP) was in play for a major campaign and activation with the same group. The powers that be may have deemed me done in that market but in my mind, my wife's company could still make a bid on the business. The key players on the regional level were aware of Diann's exquisite capabilities, as she had worked with them prior as well. When it was time to make the bid, I jumped on it. Note, I used my wife's company to engage in a consulting agreement with another group within Nike where I was the key man. The consulting agreement was on a global level while the RFP was on a regional level. Just to cover my butt, I informed the global and regional leads of the desire to bid on the RFP. I obtained approval to do so and my wife's company won the business. The project was rugged to say the least.

Pushed Out of Frame

During the project, the category marketing lead accepted a new position in another market. The #2 category marketing person was not awarded the job and understandably drifted away from the business a bit. The new category marketing lead was transitioning from halfway across the country. And, the one person at Nike assigned to keep the project moving simply did not have the expertise, tactical capabilities or leadership skills to do so effectively. No problem. Wifey's company has been in tougher situations. However, midway through the project, my father-in-law became very sick and passed away. This unexpectedly threw a wrench into production. Not because we couldn't handle it, but because Nike had concerns. One would think that I would be allowed to easily step in and assist my wife and business partner given that I had done so for many Nike executives and employees over the years. No! The reason that I was not considered to be the lead and agency of record in this market prior was because of one key person that seemingly carried tons of weight. To this day I still do not understand how or why this person had it out for me. When my wife's company was awarded the business, I was told by this person that under no uncertain terms, I was not to be part of the account team. Even though

I was consulting up the food chain with two global teams and leading a project for Nike Sports marketing at the time, I was told not to show my face in this city. And, my right hand basketball operations guy Lincoln, who was running the Nike Sports marketing project at the time, was not allowed to show his face in the city either. It was obvious, the lead events person in this market was intimidated. Her peers and my staff knew it. No one at Nike on a local or national level discussed the issue with this woman. She was allowed to essentially 'bully' my company and organization. She wielded the white privilege big time and no one stopped her. So when she let everyone know I was not to be involved in the project, everyone was simply in compliance. That applied to me as well as my #2 guy Lincoln, who she had a problem with as well. There was some history here but this matter concerned the death of a parent and the appropriate accommodations should have been made for the progression of the project. There was a visceral fear of me filling in and the Nike system stood behind the hypocrisy, discriminatory spoken not written decision making. Potential failure, shortcomings, and mediocracy was the risk here but still the systems, isms and privilege was in full effect. I could not see this happening to a non-Black person, especially the silence of consensus in the market and Nike world headquarters. Furthermore, there was absolutely no remorse, empathy or compassion shown for human life or for a person losing a parent. Nevertheless, we completed the project and despite the bumps in the road it was deemed a success. But, I knew *I* was finally done with Nike. I was over it. To this day, I do not even mention Nike in my home or around my wife.

To add insult to injury, one year later there was another RFP for a similar activation. My wife was informed that her company would not be invited to respond to the RFP because her company did not possess 'basketball expertise'. My wife wasn't too concerned as she was hosting a television show in Rome at the time. She knew it was some bullcrap anyway. As for me, I needed a real answer and appropriate narrative on the matter. Think about it, at this point I had spent decades crafting award-winning programs on four continents. I had worked on countless projects within the basketball category and with Michael Jordan, LeBron James, Kobe Bryant and other high profile global, regional and local players...and all the demands of excellence that come along with working on projects with those icons. Yet, a company I own 50% of does not have basketball expertise? Now that was a punch in the mouth!

In Rome with my wife, I immediately called the key decision maker in the market. That person, who was new to the job, gave me the same corporate line about 'basketball expertise'. I explained that I did not mind not being invited to bid on the business. After the last experience, I could not stomach it. At that point, the system, isms and privilege were still working overtime for that one 'protected' individual as well as for the other agencies. I got it. What I did not appreciate was the backhanded way of demeaning my brand. Also, this was clearly a case of pencil whipping by stating why the incumbent agency that has done exemplary work for other areas of the company would not be extended at least an invitation to respond to the RFP. If you work in Corporate America and you know the game of systems, isms and privilege, you know there are far better diabolical techniques to use. It has been done to non-general market agencies for decades. At least go through the motions of allowing my wife's agency to respond...then award your friends the gig. The key decision maker was someone I had history with on a couple of Nike projects. Oddly enough, a year prior, this person put me on a plane to support one of her international colleagues to tighten up, of all things, basketball activation. When I shared with the key decision maker that I would not want to hear this narrative circulating and I have my own story about the entire situation in that marketplace, the conversation shifted to me extending a threat. Hey, mission accomplished–well played. That definitely backed me down. It would be too easy for the moniker to stick that I was the 'angry Black man'. That was and is not me at all. I would much rather eat a false claim than a character assassination that I threatened someone as that could go viral. We patched things up by the time the conversation ended. It was still some bullcrap, but I was on a street corner in Rome talking about the past when I had so much future ahead of me. I was content knowing that I had shared my thoughts. I heard from other sources about the conversation, so it did go viral as it rippled through other markets. No surprise. It's all part of the game. I was already over that ratchet and heinous treatment. It was confirmation that my time had passed with The Swoosh.

The last resounding Nike death knell was delivered by two global teams that had approached me to work with them to form a bridge and a 'center of excellence' for the two groups. The leader of one of the groups was the mastermind behind the exploration. He was a strategist and had worked around the world in a variety of functions. He was a big thinker...and maybe too blue sky for his group. Six months into my consultancy, he transitioned from Nike to a new pursuit in Silicon Valley. When he left Nike, I truly lost a champion. I was not alone. Within a couple of months, everyone he had brought in was on the chopping block. I managed to remain based on my duality of serving two groups. Without his leadership, the 'center of excellence' idea died when he left. I can recall one of my colleagues within the category telling me, "Damon, I just want to work on logistics. I do not want to be involved with the strategy stuff." This colleague was considered a young talent in the group. This sentiment typified that group's culture. Within the group, it was blue sky thinking, administration, making sure fonts were perfect on presentations. When push comes to shove, I prefer being on the ground, hands getting dirty with the people that must make things happen. Make no mistake, I can strategize with the best of them. But this globe work was a tricky game in terms of cliques, face time and making friends at all costs. One group was glad to see the leader depart, and the other group was disjointed. No togetherness or cohesive culture. When you hear the term 'global this' or 'global that' like on LinkedIn or in someone's title, you would think 'wow, that's impressive,' but in this particular case it was underwhelming. A couple of the assignments were fine... a couple of problems solved and advanced some of the global initiatives. Then, with about 25% remaining on my contract, the person that replaced my champion shared that there was no funding to fulfill my remaining contract. I could not believe that the Nike system would send in a newly hired person to deliver this message. Not to mention the idea that after all my years of blood, guts and tears, no one person or collective would tell this newbie, "We got him." It hurt even more when the newbie said, "Damon, you have such a great reputation. I hear nothing but glowing remarks about your contribution to the brand"...and all the niceties. More system bullcrap. I immediately called the other global lead who asked me to fulfill this hybrid role. Crickets. No call back from messages left on the work and mobile phone. No returned emails. No returned response for handwritten letters. Nothing. Pure cowardice. To this day I have not heard from this person. And, this is from a person whose boss left her with me during her first week or month on the job. I was the lead on a major project but still fulfilled the role of training up a new Nike employee for a dear friend. This person and I had a long history, but not enough. I also shared with about twenty-five Nike employees that I was under financial duress due to Nike shorting me on a contract. I received two responses. Both wanting to know more about the details than actually assisting me. This let me know when you're off The Swoosh boat you are truly off the boat, back turned. No one cares that you are drowning either. And, you better swim fast before someone makes you catch the anchor. Man, my long, glorious run at Nike was truly over in a cold, heartless manner.

My goal is not to smash Nike. I cannot front, I had some great years and times with The Swoosh, but this is a narrative to share how things came to an end for me. I am thankful that this gruesome treatment and the lack of consideration did not come on the front end of my experience as I know plenty of former Nike employees, consultants and contractors that were treated as such and/or did not last as long as I did. In the end, everything was fair game as people are entitled to their opinions, evoking the fine print on a contract to wiggle out of an agreement and turning their back on a relationship. Plus, at the time of these unfortunate occurrences, Nike did not define me. Nor does Nike get credit for shaping my business acumen and talent. I knew the game from learning over the years, so I always made sure I had my big boy pants on and braced myself for the punch in the mouth just in case.

My strategy has always been to diversify my earnings, my life's passion and my career portfolio. But one thing for sure, sports opportunities were transforming for me. I had a less than desirable end to a phenomenal, life-changing run doing work in China as well. I worked on a project for eight months only to be demoted by the category lead one day prior to the culmination of the project. It felt like a knife to my heart as I started the project journey with a comrade who passed away suddenly in the midst of the project. One of the greatest moments I have had in life was getting a call from the GM of the business unit informing me that the project won Nike's highest honor. I was truly proud I could deliver excellence for my friend, but I knew my China run would be over. The call mended my injured heart. The lead that demoted me was also good friends with the owner of an agency I was consulting with. We did great work with Nike Greater China, NFL China and Kobe Bryant. My contract was not renewed and I have not been back to China on work since then. I worked with the management teams of Michael Jordan, LeBron James and Kobe Bryant. After a long run working with Michael Jordan Flight Schools, MJ ceased doing his fantasy camp in Las Vegas and my run at his youth camp in Santa Barbara was over. I was a fixture in LeBron's circle as I ran his camp, worked with some of his endorsement partners and ran his bikeathon. LeBron ceased doing his bikeathon as well as his camps and I stopped getting calls from his management team to work on or consult on projects. With respect to Kobe, he was right in my backyard of Los Angeles. We shared a love for China and I had Michigan ties to his agent. However, I was not dialed into his business enterprise. I was able to help on a few LA projects and deliver a China deal, but I did not work consistently with his team per se. At the time, these 'misses' puzzled me. Once again, I can only believe that I did not have the right 'ingredients' for their recipes. Maybe I was not qualified. Maybe I did not possess the capabilities. Maybe I did not deliver enough

THE BOOK OF DH

value. Maybe I was not a proper fit. Or simply, I was not worthy of any positions those guys sought to escalate their business enterprises. In any event, as time progressed, my time was done with those guys, too.

Moving on, I knew a couple of former Nike employees that had landed over at Adidas. They were striving to pull me in as a consultant. They knew what I was capable of and the project entailed some strategies, campaigns and activations I had done countless times over the years. One of the executives at the top of the food chain was a former Nike employee, but I had to work through a director level lead to secure the consultancy. The director level lead was in Los Angeles so we met over dinner. We hit it off immediately, as the dinner lasted a couple of hours. I offered the lead a ride back to the hotel. At his hotel, I decided to go all in. We posted up at a table at the bar and I whipped out my computer and shared with him project after project I had worked on. He was sold on my capabilities. A few weeks passed and I checked in with him. We had the usual small talk, then he shared that he believed that I was the right choice to lead his project. He commenced to change his tone and asked me straight up if I had an issue with the top person in his organization that was formerly at Nike. I said, "No, not that I am aware of." He stated that he was perplexed that with all the other talent that was being secured by this particular executive that I would not be part of the marketing mix. I had three other people championing my cause and it still wasn't enough to move the needle favorably for me. Coincidently, a human resource representative called me soon after my Adidas consultancy conversation vanished. The human resource representative outlined a full-time job opportunity. During the course of the conversation, I provided insights to Adidas athletes, strategies and point of views on the roles and responsibilities for the job. The Adidas HR rep stated at one point during the conversation, "You should have been in a meeting we had just last week!" The HR rep asked about my availability for flying in for an interview. He shared with me whom I would be interviewing with. Of course, the top executive was the same former Nike employee that stonewalled me for the consultancy. I shared with the HR rep before he advocated too hard for me that he should only mention our conversation with his boss. I offered that upon soft selling me, if there is support send me available times for an interview. If the boss does not support me in this position, then send me a generic 'thanks but no thanks' email and close this file accordingly. The HR rep kept his word. By the end of the week, I had the generic rejection letter. I then knew Adidas was not an option for me and my sports opportunities had shrunken even more.

I worked on small scale consulting gigs and I even found myself back at Troika as its Head of Sports marketing. The president Dan had called me and asked if I would be interested in coming back, as he had received funding from new investors and the business would be fortified and poised for hyper growth. He had always been a great leader, out of the box thinker and a genuine guy so I returned. My tenure there was short lived. In essence, the new management team had ideas of utilizing funds to grow through acquisition, making the culture very nebulous and tough to align with. To my surprise, there was not a significant investment to grow sports marketing. Also, I could not get on the same page with my director on a number of fronts. Funny, the first time he invited me to lunch was on my last day on the job. The sports marketing world of opportunities had shrunk even more for me. Then one day, I received a call from an executive talent recruiter, Carolina, from Under Armour (UA). We had met before as the #2 guy at UA had flown me in for informational interviews to meet with six VPs. The interviews went well and she kept me in mind. We discussed a position to be the General Manager of Steph Curry's brand. Similar to Michael Jordan and Nike, this brand would serve as a subsidiary of UA. I was immediately intrigued. UA was a small player in the game but still a $5 billion dollar company. The founder Kevin Plank was somewhat of a living legend. He was young, enterprising and a billionaire. Steph was off the charts, too. Mr. Unanimous MVP of the NBA, best shooter of all time with a great underdog story. Plus, he played in the Bay Area which provided extra incentive for me to win in that marketplace for the greater good of all parties involved. Carolina, one of the finest human resource professionals I have ever known. She tested me, grilled me and prepared me for the internal discussions. She knew my heart was in it so she gave me excellent ideas, insights and concepts to consider. After Carolina, I talked to the hiring manager Kevin, who was one of the top executives at UA. We had an authentic connection. He did not 'mail it in' as he was inquisitive, probed appropriately and was curious about my vast experience. Then, I met Bryant, the head of Steph's company SC30. As you can imagine, Steph has numerous business pursuits. SC30 was responsible for the UA relationship. We had a face-to-face meeting in Los Angeles. Bryant was sharp, purposeful, to the point and kept the conversation flowing. We covered a lot of ground and I felt even better about the opportunity. Carolina called soon after and extended an offer for me to have on-site interviews at UA world headquarters. I felt an energy, a vibe that I had not felt in a long time. I asked Diann for permission to move to Baltimore if I were to accept the job. Of course, she said yes like she always does. As long as there is great shopping, she is down for whatever.

I can honestly say I have never studied more for an interview than I did for this one. I had to understand Kevin Plank, Patrik Frisk the president, the UA business, Steph's UA product line and business as well as UA Basketball overall. I remember the interview day vividly because it was my mom's birthday. I did not tell her about the interview but my big brother, Eric, knew and told me jokingly if I am missing Mom's birthday, I better get the job. I met with the top brass of UA that day. Of course, Steph Curry is their most prized athlete. The cornerstone interview of the morning was with Patrik, a smart Swedish gentleman, stockholder value and operations guy. I had my wall street friend Phil work up a one-pager on what made him successful with fashion brands. The cornerstone of the afternoon was Kevin Plank. It is not too many times you will sit across the table from a dynamic, game changing, go-getter like him. The first half of the interview he came at me. The second half I went at him, smiles and laughs but real talk the whole time. I loved his energy. At the end of the interview, I looked him in the eye and told him I am the guy for this job and I would not let him down. I dusted off my Michigan MBA interview training and my girl Val's line to ask for the job if things go well in the interview. When I left, his administrative assistant shared that KP must have liked me as he usually does not talk to people that long. I felt even better.

About a week later, Carolina called to share that I had made it to the next level and that I would be meeting with the man himself...Steph. I knew from the beginning that Steph would only be meeting with finalists so I knew I was close and truly in the running. I was scheduled to have dinner with Steph and Bryant. Steph was in season so I had to meet him on the road. Fortunately, my guy Roe Goldstein was a resident in that city. I arrived early to spend time with him. His nickname is 'The Closer' so it was good energy to be in his aura hours before meeting Steph. I met him and Bryant at a great Italian restaurant. I was more at ease given my familiarity with the cuisine and culture. We shut the place down. We talked about him, me, footwear, marketing, the state of the business, family, the Bay Area and more. We were at the same hotel and said our goodbyes in the elevator as his floor was above mine.

Steph is a great guy. Over dinner he was mellow, calm and soft spoken–much different from other NBA guys I have sat across from such as Earvin, Michael, LeBron and Kobe. Those other guys...well not so much. Above all, I thought I had a good chance. Hey, I was a finalist so I at least had a 50/50 chance. I racked my brain trying to increase my chances anyway...at least in my mind.

The final decision took an extraordinarily long time. Carolina, the consummate professional, kept me well informed that no decision had been made on a regular basis. I was a bit nervous because I knew some former Nike employees that were then employed by UA and they were chirping in my ear. I knew the competition. Similar to me, that person had engaged in informational interviews at UA in the past as well. UA knew both of us quite well. Also, similar to me, he had a personal brand and reputation within the footwear industry. The more time elapsed, my nervousness subsided and my mind was on to something else. Then, one day I received a call from Carolina. She dropped a bomb on me. I was not chosen to be the GM of the SC30 Brand. She said all the right things about my candidacy and my performance during the interview process. No disrespect to Carolina at all, but all I heard was blah, blah, blah. I asked for the real feedback and how I lost it or how I got beat. Her response was that during the assessment of the finalists for the GM position, the criteria changed in that it was deemed UA needed someone with footwear design experience. Damn! This was a new one: moving the target and changing the rules in the middle of the game. Damn! Oh, did I already say that? I was actually speechless. All parties in the process knew who I was on paper, in person and the skill set I brought as a GM as well as the strengths of the other candidate. What seemed odd was that this role reported to the Head of Footwear Design? So I was even more confused, disgusted and, actually, defeated. So, in essence, I felt the game was changed to accommodate the other candidate. If I was on the ropes prior to this UA experience with respect to my future in sports, this was definitely the knockout punch. The saving grace was that I was in Las Vegas with my moms and brother Eric when I spoke to Carolina, so I was able to take my mind off the devastating blow. The following week, and what made this news and experience worse were the 3 to 4 calls I received from UA employees. I learned that there was a bit of an internal struggle in making this decision. To restate what I heard lightly, there was some bias, unfairness and pencil whipping in play as it pertains to the decision. Painful but not surprising. And, after competing for such a high position, I did not hear anything from the hiring manager, Kevin, or SC30 president, Bryant. Poof! It was as if I had disappeared like I was not even in Baltimore with UA having me take a tour of the city to look for housing, or meeting with Bryant twice during the process.

| 131 |

Soon after the footwear world had heard about UA's decision, I received a number of disparaging calls regarding UA's choice. The calls were nice to receive as it is always good for people to share their thoughts, sympathize with my scenario and affirm my worth. But in the end, I did not complete my mission and receive the job offer, so the talk was just more blah, blah, blah. I actually did not care about the other candidate and their journey, competency, past performance, reputation or projections of their performance in the job, or UA's practices, culture, industry reputation and shortcomings. I lost. I did not get the job. That person had the right ingredients to make their recipe better than mine in the eyes of UA and Steph. That person had the straw that broke through to UA and Steph leadership to get the nod. I had been rebuked from a number of groups within Nike and possibly with a tarnished name. I was not going to get any looks from Adidas or any other footwear company. I had put my name in the hat with the NBA, MLB and NFL but received no responses. I was not in the consideration set of athletes or sports executives I had worked with in the past. The end was staring me in the face. Sports and Damon Haley may be over.

Key Takeaways

- In the service business, unless you have an undeniable bundle of talent or you are integrated into the corporate leadership structure, you will face the end of the relationship at some point. Diversify your client list and always plan an exit or transition strategy.

- If you love an industry, exhaust every resource you can to remain a part of it before you decide to make a transition.

- Remember, it is business…not personal. Knowing this will help you stay unbothered by external conditions, no matter what happens.

10

Hold Up, the Party is Not Over

> *I'm a Savage! I'm a Savage! I'm a Savage! Whatever I want, I'm going to get! Whatever I want, I have to get! What's next?!*
>
> SEAN "PUFFY' COMBS

Admittedly, I tend to pivot quickly when it comes to major disappointments in my professional career. When I was passed over for the Bermuda position at Chevron, I pivoted from finance to marketing. When I experienced a lack of upward mobility and was offered a few subpar offers at Nike, I pivoted to launch UMCA. When I was burned out with UMCA, I quickly gravitated toward consulting. With the UA Steph general manager situation, I was placing sports in my rearview mirror. I will admit, I took this one pretty hard. In my quest for the position, I delved into UA. I figured with my experience and UA having no significant presence in China, minimal street credibility in the USA, thirst for a jolt in the basketball category and a desperate need of diversity, I thought I would be a good choice over the skill sets of the person that was hired. From Steph's and SC30's perspective, once I was the GM on UA's dime I would be part of the team and bring all my might to Steph's growing empire. Plus, Steph's positioning was that he was the cool suburban guy. The market demand to grow the business unit would have been to give his brand a little metropolitan swag. Once again, I live, breathe and eat this kind of stuff. But hey, that is what I get for thinking too much. All the while I thought I had a good 50/50 chance. In the end, the game revealed I was wrong and my chances may have been nil going into the interview process. And that truly made me think "Wow, I hit rock bottom in the sports game."

Entrepreneurship: A Pivotal Shift to a Whole New Path

I pivoted, shifted, and all that new wave verbiage. I gained strength and inspiration from my interview with Kevin Plank. I was truly uplifted from our engagement. He evaluated me but I studied his words as he shared his story and future pursuits. He was a regular guy, he was a grinder. He used grit, hustle and will to build a multibillion dollar company. And, despite the pressures he may have been under, he was having fun building hotels, breweries and his hobby-type business empire outside of UA. Similar to my experience interviewing with Magic eons ago, I was not Kevin's 'guy' but I was a guy that was in the running for something unique and special. So I decided that I did not need permission in the form of being hired to build something new and extraordinary. Doors had been shut, closed and boarded up for me. I was not good enough anyway for the sports space, right? I know it is not all true, but I had to use mantras like this to 'exorcise' sports out of my system to make way for something else. The search was on for my future.

It did not take me long to decide on being an entrepreneur. I was an agency owner but from a pure service side of the business. This foyer would be driven by products and a system that was driven by consumer demand. I had failed at client demand for my services. One day, I was at my favorite bakery, Nothing Bundt Cake, and I noticed a delivery. I began to think, "Wow, this business is about adding water, stirring and adding sugar on top." I was determined to buy a franchise or two. I went through the process. It was phenomenal information, understanding the franchise system and business modeling. I wanted to obtain a location in the heart of Los Angeles, but was not granted the rights to do so. The corporate office came back to offer a location hours from Los Angeles. My wife and I met with the owners, we crunched the numbers and strongly considered moving. In the end, we could not make the numbers work and had serious second thoughts of maintaining two homes in Southern California. The juice simply was not worth the squeeze. Still, we kept looking for bakeries and met with a few independent owners but could not get the right deal done.

The other industry that called to me was beauty supplies. I had a great sense of a 'house of brands' retail environment and I knew the beauty industry never sleeps. It is recession-proof and all that sensible thinking, but I knew in my heart of hearts women care about all things beauty all the time. Plus, looking at my master bathroom countertop, the jam-packed drawers under the bathroom sink, and my wife's vanity area of the bathroom, I knew beauty supply stores could be a viable investment venture. Upon looking at a few opportunities, I saw one that piqued my interest. I drove about 90 minutes to a business broker's office to hash through the numbers. My MBA and Chevron experience came in handy. After the meeting with the brokers, we decided to move forward with the exploration which included an on-site visit to meet the owner of the store. The broker gave me the address. Funny enough, I drove 90 minutes to find a beauty supply store that was 10 minutes from my childhood home. When I saw the address, I knew exactly where the store was located. I shared with the broker that my go-to fish joint was two doors down from the beauty supply store and the Ralph's across the street is where I shop for my moms. Small world, literally and geographically. We met with the owner and we began negotiations on the purchase. I thought to myself that I had been around the world, working with global brands and iconic people all to come back to my neighborhood and set up shop. A pivot indeed.

Soon after the beauty supply deal was in progress, my wife received an offer to purchase a hair extension studio in an affluent neighborhood in Los Angeles. My wife designed the space and knew the owner well. She believed that the business would be a great investment for us. All of sudden, I was 'all in' on beauty. Growing up in a family with three boys, a manly pops, and a mother with five brothers as well as working in sports for decades, I clearly moved from a male-dominated environment to a female space. I am not sure what the most extreme word for 'pivot' is, but that is what I did. The beauty salon business was acquired before the beauty supply store deal was done. Being antifragile on a daily basis was an understatement, I jumped into the business aspects as the point of sale and customer relationship manager system as well as working with the incumbent accountant. I also worked closely with the newly hired salon manager to develop standard operating procedures so everyone was aligned. Everything was new for me so most of this stuff was for me to learn and catch up with everyone else. I will spare the stories of how I became familiar with hair, hairstyles, hair products and all things women. It was now my business and life so I needed to enjoy the ride. When the beauty supply store deal closed, I jumped into that as well. There were more moving parts with that business in terms of distributors, manufacturers, inventory, staffing and monitoring the business closely. It was a lot to uncover, discover, learn, process and perfect. It was like drinking water out of a fire hydrant...and still is.

Rebranding Beauty Supply: New Avenue, Same Skill Sets

As you may be aware, Koreans dominate the Black beauty supply space in the USA. Their dominance has been for the last fifty years or so. There has been a tenuous relationship with Black people and Korean people over the years. Koreans have also dominated liquor and dollar stores, fish markets, fried chicken fast-food restaurants, donut shops and cleaners in Black neighborhoods. Note: the 'why' around this is a more extensive conversation. With respect to the beauty supply industry, it is well documented that Koreans have discriminated against Black consumers, beauty supply store owners and product manufacturers. You can find stories in every major market in the USA on this topic. Some of these stories sadly are true and others are false with the truth somewhere in between. In my case, I did not experience any negativity associated with the purchase of my beauty supply store. The previous owner, Leo, was magnificent in his support during our transition. He provided a 'white glove' introduction to his suppliers and manufacturers. I trained with him for a month and I truly believe he gave me everything he had to give. He was a tough negotiator but that was all business, not racial or personal. He wanted me, my wife and our community to win. I even offered him to come back and assist me with major inventory orders, year-end protocols, and to discuss other acquisition targets. He was gracious with his time and wisdom across the board. In essence, not only were there no horror stories here, but Leo was an upstanding businessman and will remain a lifelong friend.

The first thing we did with both businesses was a total rebrand process. I used the same game plan I would utilize if I were brought into a sports or entertainment project. We looked at the consumer and injected aspiration, good vibes and the 'North Star' of one's best self. The result? We created the Glow + Flow Beauty Brand. #BeautyIsYourBestAccessory, #GlowGirl, The Glow...It's Your Power, Is Ya Glowin' or is Ya Flowin' are some of our branded statements we use to energize our clients, customers and environment. We created a consistent color palette of gold, gray and white with a distinctive and clear look to the logo. We went contrary to the existing Korean beauty supply model...no pink, no hair models, no outdated creative, only interesting patterns and a fresh clean look. My boy, Ray, the G.O.A.T of all things brand design would be proud. We also built out our social media, website, and created our own tribe called 'Glow Getters'. Funny, all my old friends that visit our locations or customer/client events make comments likening the environments to what I did for HBO, Nike, Paramount, Lionsgate and other clients...and they are right. Glow + Flow is just the 5.0 version of all the stuff I had done in the past. All of my skills are constantly put to the test in my current role as an entrepreneur of two businesses and we also maintain my wife's event production and design agency. As of today, we own our beauty supply store; are in escrow for a second location; and looking for a third Los Angeles location. We have also registered for Glow + Flow Franchises with interested buyers in North and South Carolina as well as Texas. Soon we are launching our own line of synthetic hair and beauty supply products. And the party ain't over, it is just beginning!

I could not believe that after one year of receiving truly devastating news that nudged me out of sports, I was able to rebound by taking on a totally different industry where we know hurdles and obstacles exist. And guess what, I made a comeback! I am an equity partner in Hoop Dreams–a lifestyle and social impact company. My co-owners are actor Michael B. Jordan and NBA Player Kyrie Irving. Also, I am an equity partner in Phenom Consulting Group–a multi-disciplinary marketing consultancy assembled to Build, Accelerate and Power Businesses with fresh, thoughtful marketing ideas and actions. My partners are long time friends, brothers and Nike colleagues Ray Butts and Brandon Nicholson. The lesson in all of this? Transformation. I am back at it!

I guess that's what I do. Just like being the youngest kid in a family of five got me street-ready; understanding the systems, isms and privilege through my education, corporate life and agency ownership has gotten me razor-sharp for this game. I hope that I never experience what I endured in terms of the bullcrap of being a hard-driving, excellence seeking, high performing Black man dealing with and navigating public schools and universities or Corporate America, but time will tell. God has blessed me with some serious direction and favor. I relish the idea of my story and journey inspiring others. I hope that you are encouraged and motivated by my story. Despite the negative forces you may face in your life, I believe that where there's a will, there's a way.

The world is not fair at all, but *you* can be fair and true to yourself. Do what you feel is right. Be antifragile. Do not let anyone break you. Do not let your momentum pause, keep moving and doing the damn thing. Always believe in yourself and your abilities. And, most of all, always pursue and shout out loud: DREAMS & HOPES, BABY!

Key Takeaways

- Develop and cultivate your transferable skills. Keep a running tab of how many tools you have and can utilize. If all you have is a hammer, then act as if everything is a nail. Stay overqualified to do it all.

- Don't be boxed in. Believe that you have the power to succeed in anything you choose to do in life. Don't stop, won't stop, can't stop should be a part of your mindset.

- If you claim to be about business, buy one, buy two, or own a few. In the end, if the businesses are successful you can then do whatever you want to do!

MY DAD AND ME

Bonus Chapter

My dad's passing was a big blow to my life. A dude that was there all the time for me was no longer there. I was deeply saddened. As therapy, I wrote about him. This chapter is a collection of my life lessons and experiences with him. I affectionately call it 'Robert Lee's Rules of Order' as a play on words to the parliamentary procedures called Robert's Rules of Order. My dad was about efficiency, productivity and, of course, order. On the flip side, he was fun-loving, joyous, bodacious and boisterous at times as well as a loving, kind man. You have read about my experiences in my neighborhood, on campuses and at my places of work. This chapter provides insights into my life at home with my dad...the man who nurtured me, crafted me, and engineered me.

PLACE YOUR BETS

They say that you can choose your friends but you cannot choose your family. You are born into a family by the favor of God. Well, God favored me from the start of my life by blessing me with Robert Lee Haley. I believe in the concept of nature, nurture and nativity. When I was conceived, I received some gifts from my moms and pops: DNA, genetics, etc. (nature). God gave me gifts as well (nativity). Along my path of growth, maturity, development and life, I received gifts (nurture). I appreciate the combination of all of my gifts and talents. I was fortunate to spend 47 years with Dad and I give him credit for shaping me into the man I am today.

MY DAD AND ME

My pops spent his early years in Tennessee and Ohio, and after high school went to the army. After his military service, he went to college for three years then moved to California and worked for the County of Los Angeles for 27 years. He retired at age 52, lived in the same house for 50+ years, bought 3 cars during his lifetime and his vacations consisted of hunting, fishing and 'Weekend Vegas Runs'. He raised 5 children (four boys) in South Central LA, was married to my moms for 50+ years until his death and was a cornerstone on 'the block' among our neighbors. He regularly got tipsy, smoked cigarettes and cigars and loved, loved, loved every part of the pig. It would demean him to say he was simple, but he led a simple life. He was rich with happiness, resolve, respect, friends and family. He worked at it, although it seemed effortless to him. His 'flow' was such that people gravitated to and believed in him. He was a devoted friend, supporter and confidant. He was great with his hands and could fix anything. Imagine a garage full of nothing but tools and hardware supplies. It was heaven on earth to him. He converted that garage into a 'clubhouse' for him and his friends until his dying days. Once again, simple. To build a life around a South Central LA community, a growing family, old and new friends, and life dynamics, nothing is further than his truth of simplicity. He remained simple as the culture, neighborhood, family and changing social, political and economic environment around him became complex.

My dad was a 'transformative old school' dude. The core of him was old school, but he was totally open to new thoughts, ideas and concepts. At the very least, my dad would look, listen and learn. But most of the time he would elect to support and/or conform to his personal preference. All the while, being cool, 'okay' and supportive with one doing their 'own thing'. He talked a lot of s@#$ and let you know what he thought, but he would never ever want or advocate for you to do things other than your way. He believed 100% in you being yourself and furthering your talents and abilities. His most powerful phrases to me would be in the form of challenging questions. The most prevalent would be "What do you think?." His questioning was always rhetorical or sarcastic. I began to understand the idea of being rhetorical and sarcastic as I began to grow. I knew that his questions were not implying right, wrong or an attempt of shifting opinion, but more so thought-provoking to enable better clarity, justification, rationale, belief, confidence that I would have in my positions. After I learned this, I sought out conversations and discussions with him on a variety of topics. I never feared conversing with my pops about anything. We were cool like that. I knew in the end, he was my #1 supporter regardless of what I was doing, thought, envisioned or sought out to do.

PLAY AT YOUR OWN RISK

I loved and adored my dad. In an era when African American fathers were thought to not have a presence in homes, communities and in the lives of sons and daughters, my dad was the complete opposite. He was engaged, active, inquisitive and always present. He was not overbearing per se, but he always had an opinion if something was not right or in excellence...and he taught me those were two different things. If there is right and wrong, then there is 'half ass' and excellent. My pops furiously, viciously and aggressively attacked wrong and half-ass activities, efforts and results. To this day, his nudges and prods stimulate me to be 100% precise, clear, detailed and purposeful in my daily routine and flow.

Growing up the youngest of five, my guess is that my dad had enough practice at fatherhood by the time I came around. I was also his fourth boy (my sister was the middle child). He knew what was a real and actionable concern, problem or issue and what wasn't. I think as long as I was not killing myself or anyone else or destroying property, all was good. In the spirit of the chicken or the egg, I am not sure which came first—my risk taking, 'unfiltered-ness' and pushing limits or my dad's laissez-faire approach that allowed me to test parameters. I am certain that my brothers had it a little different based on birth order, parental maturity, finances, etc., but I am sure that pops was consistent with the way he went about managing the household, his children and

MY DAD AND ME

the surrounding environment. My dad taught me a couple of things early in life about 'how he rolls'. When I think of the lessons taught by my pops, I affectionately refer to them as 'Robert Lee's Rules of Order'. This was a simple set of rules that existed around 2145 (our family home growing up). My dad was a fair man. You could do whatever you wanted except 'cross the line'. He cared primarily about 'the line'. There were a number of specific rules, but he made life simple. Do what you are told. Do your job. Do your best. If you don't do these things, you better have a damn good reason and not a weak excuse. And also, do what you want, be it good, bad, right or wrong but be prepared for any blowback.

My first recollection of Robert Lee's Rules of Order occurred in the midst of a torture session by my youngest big brother. My moms and pops left me, my youngest brother and sister at 2145 one Saturday. My moms left a 'laundry list' of duties. Typical protocol around 2145 was when the work is done you get your freedom. My brother had tasked me to do a couple of simple duties on the list. Thinking that I had done them, my brother left the house for the day. I failed to empty the paper trash cans in each room of the house. When my pops returned, I noticed that he went hard on my siblings. I thought it was funny in a little brother type of way. Needless to say, pops passed out some punishment to my brother and sister. After which, my brother commenced to the torture session in the backyard...intolerable pain, irritation, etc. and more so than usual big brother on little brother torture. Then, when my dad heard my screams and came outside, I thought for sure it was for rescue. The action stopped but positions stayed the same with my brother on top of me and controlling me. My brother explained to pops why he was beating me. My dad's response, "Keep the noise down." That was a major reality check for me. He did not stop my brother from pouncing on me, did not monitor the degree of torture or administer the punishment himself. The experience let me - 'the baby' - know, the 'favorite child' was not immune to penalty, ramifications and repercussions from not following instructions around 2145. I learned early to do the task at hand...period, or, suffer with little mercy. Anything less than getting the job done, then you succumb to the system of structure and to those that are bigger and stronger than you. A very simple but powerful lesson to learn, as I was the youngest of five with a long time to go before I was big enough to deal with and handle issues in the 'backyard' of life.

The 2145 backyard served as the ultimate classroom in my life with my dad as the professor. Unlike today's youth, I spent 95% of my waking hours outside. Whether it was playing on my block, down the street, or around the corner or at the park, I was outside until the street lights came on. When I was growing up, my dad gave me specific instructions - be in before the streetlights came on. On many occasions, I followed the instructions...and when I did not there was a grace period. Then one day, I came home and all the doors were locked. I rang the doorbell. My dad answered. His words were simple. He calmly said, "I told you to be in before the streetlights came on". Then, he pointed to the nearest street light, which was lit. I thought it was a joke and that he couldn't possibly be serious. I could hear my moms politicking for me to be allowed to come in the house. When she succumbed, I knew he wasn't joking. He told me I was sleeping in the garage, which is detached from the house and in the backyard. With no place to go, I went to the garage. A little later that evening, I heard the backdoor open. I thought the joke was over. Nope. Pops brought me dinner. He had a really big smile on his face. He liked stuff like this. We talked for a little while then he went back into the house. He came back outside again, and I thought the joke was over. Nope. He fed the dog and took my dishes back into the house. I was pissed off, confused, crying, cursing at him (where he could not hear, of course) and had time to think long and hard. Freedom and flexibility has responsibility. Privileges can be revoked. Know the rules. Follow the rules. Be disciplined. Don't slip. One night was all it took for me to apply this to my life. I only spent one night in any garage, figuratively or literally.

MY DAD AND ME

I grew up with a dog named Bo. He was brought to 2145 as a puppy when I was 2 years old. Early on, my dad was Bo's primary caregiver so to speak. As I grew up, Bo became my 'job' and sole responsibility. I fed, bathed, walked and cleaned up the yard behind him. One day, Bo tore through a trash bag and scattered trash all around the backyard. Pops was pissed. When my pops got pissed off, he didn't raise his voice. But he talked, gritting his teeth. And he always started the sentence with "God Dammit". Actually, he said that a couple of times throughout too. When my pops saw this, he grabbed Bo, put his head in the trash bag and whipped him. I thought it was cruel. Pops was steaming. Then he turned to me and said, "God Dammit, clean this s@#$ up". Just when I thought all was cool and the scenario had passed. Later on when I went into the kitchen to grab a bite to eat, my dad said "What are you doing?" I told him, "Getting something to eat." He calmly said "You aren't eating." He then explained that the reason Bo went into the trash is because I did not feed him and that I would suffer the same fate. I attempted to defend myself by making excuses. His level of 'pissed-offness' shot through the roof. All I remember is me not going anywhere or eating that day and most of the next day, which seemed like an eternity. I was desperate and hungry. My pops caught me eating in the backyard. I had snuck some food outside. I thought he was going to erupt. Instead, he essentially shared the lengths that one would go to when they are starving and deprived. He used this situation as an example and a huge lesson about taking care of your business, another living being, maintaining the order of 2145 and looking at cause and effect. My pops was big on cherishing what you have, opportunities, 'building and stacking' and avoiding senseless risk to jeopardize your situation. My dad gave me tons of 'rope' and always pushed me to create 'lassos' and not 'nooses'.

WIN - PLACE - SHOW

One of my dad's hobbies was horse racing. Since he liked it, I loved it as a child. I would go to the race track with him, study the horses and learn the intricacies of betting. At first, my joy was derived in just going someplace new. When there, the joy shifted to the strength, size and speed of the horses. Ultimately, it was very apparent that the energy of the race track was created by betting, winning and losing. Thus, I gravitated to that aspect and my pops entertained my interest. Of course I would add my two cents to his thinking while placing bets, then at one point he put bets down for me as well. He taught me the horse racing betting concepts of favorites, odds, studying horses' and jockeys' history and the most vital concept of all...Win - Place - Show. For me, it was like a lesson in applied mathematics and critical thinking. I actually began to win with a few of my picks. I was 'all in' and would love to go to the race track with my pops. Not to see the horses, not to see the race but to win the bets. All was good until one day my dad schooled me on my shortcomings.

To 'Win' is to come in first place. To 'Place' was to come in second place. To 'Show' was to come in third place. The 'Favorite' is the horse most likely to win based on past performance, other horses in the race, the type of track terrain, length of race, etc. I began to bet that the Favorite in the race would Show - or come in third. There are different odds and fluctuating betting cost in that the actual payoff is less when you bet on the Favorite versus a long shot. So in essence, I was betting for the best horse in the race to come in third versus first. A very safe, payoff strategy. He shared that I was leaving money on the table by not betting on the horse I thought would win to come in first as that was the optimal payoff opportunity. And, not putting more money down on it to Win, Place AND Show as monies can be won from each one of these bets was leaving money on the table as well. I quickly transformed my 'betting habits' to focus on the Win and Place and Show. More importantly, it intensified my thinking, intellectual drive, fact finding, conversation, study habits and gut feelings on betting. The betting also got 'real' when I exceeded my betting limits and my dad gave me the opportunity to bet my weekly allowance. Pops would always bait me into stuff like this. He would challenge me in that way. As for most youth, allowance was my only source of income. It only took a few bad days at the track before I learned my lesson about gambling, trusting livestock, losing money that I need for day-to-day pleasures and diversifying my modes of making money.

My dad 'fed' my betting spirit…the winning, the losing, the gaining by decision making and risk. This was prevalent and became another form of Robert Lee's Rules of Order. This rule - on the other side of winning is always losing. In college, I learned that this was an aspect of game and economic theory called 'Zero Sum Game'. By the time I was in college, I was an expert. My dad kept coins/pocket change in a five gallon water bottle in his room (Note: This is before 16 ounce to 1 liter water bottles were available at the convenient and grocery stores. Companies actually delivered 5 gallon water bottles to homes). My dad would periodically invite and challenge me to count the coins for accuracy. If I was right, then I was paid. If I was wrong, it cost me something. My dad often created the wager. Invitations and challenges like this were not just for 'fun'. There was always winning, losing and skin in the game. Growing up, my dad used to pay me for good grades. At first, it was one payoff for B's and a higher payoff for A's. Nothing for C's. By the time I was in junior and high school, A's became a win and all else was a loss. My pops taught me the art and science of 'coming strong or not coming at all'. And the knowing, not thinking, that there is distinct benefit to knowing the odds, being the favorite as well as figuratively 'working' the win, place and show payoff in all applicable situations.

This knowledge helped change the trajectory in my life when I used it to gain acceptance into business school. During the application process, I was having a hard time figuring out my personal statement - what to write, share and convey. I had a random discussion with my dad about it one day. One of those "what's new with you" type conversations. Nothing planned. No expectations. My dad thought I was overthinking it. He was puzzled why a grown man would have problems talking about himself. He simplified things in a matter of fact manner like that. It did not matter that it was a personal statement for business school. He ultimately said I should tell them who I am. I should be me. After careful consideration, then just doing it, the title of my personal statement was *I Come to Play. I Come to Win. I Come to Kick Ass.* I know the language and tonality I deployed was aggressive, unorthodox and risky, but in the end when I sealed that envelope I felt really good about 'giving them me'. Needless to say, I was accepted to business school. My pops bugged out from my personal statement when I let him read it. He was in utter disbelief that his counsel inspired my submission. It was not until the end of my first year of business school that the topic of my personal statement was revisited. I was engaged in a project with the Office of Admissions. Me, the reader of my business school application and the Director of Admissions had a good laugh from my personal statement. I was told it was unique, stood out and it was obviously memorable. Despite the language and tonality, they shared they understood my message and had a good feeling about me being a part of the student body.

DON'T WORRY ABOUT THE HORSE BEING BLIND, JUST LOAD THE F@#$&* WAGON

My dad pretty much told me and my brothers to do something once. If it was not done, he shifted right into 'judge, jury and warden mode'. My brothers were my seniors by 15, 11 and 6 years. We all shared the same experience with a weekly 2145 ritual...taking out the garbage cans. At 2145, every Wednesday was and is still 'trash day'. At one point in our lives, my brothers and I had the responsibility of taking the garbage cans from the backyard to the street for Thursday morning pick up. I was told this once and after which I was punished when I did not perform the duty. No reminders. No warnings. It was really simple. If it was not done on Wednesday, you get the penalty. And most of the time, it was on Saturday. As my brothers would attest, Pops would not say one word if the trash cans were not put out. He would do the task. But then on Saturday when you were about to leave 2145, Pops would say "Where do you think you are going". And the result would be nowhere. My dad was the king of 'if-then'. He was 'black and white' with a matter of fact type persona in laying down the law. If I introduced 'gray', he would go deep black or white. This quest for 'the gray' would only worsen the situation. There were no appeals in the world of Robert Lee's Rules of Order. The penalty would always be steeper. And I can hear him now saying, "You started this."

My dad was consistent. He was notorious for unusual punishment; especially for not being on time, not doing what you say you are going to do and not honoring Robert Lee's Rules of Order. I can recall a day at the amusement park with my siblings and cousins that ended with my brother chasing the car when he failed to be back at the parking stall at the designated time. We were all in the car waiting for my brother. My dad was calm other than his signature talking while gritting his teeth. When my brother was in sight, my dad pulled out of the parking stall. When my brother approached the car, my dad pulled off. My brother chased the car again. My dad took off. Then he would do it again. Finally, when my dad had enough, my brother jumped in the car pissed off and we all went home. My dad was funny like that. He was a master at transferring the 'pissed offness' feeling from him to you. His style was real, physical, creative, irritating and unimaginable. Another rule of order was bedtime. As a family, we did not have a bedtime per se. The only caveat was that you could not fall asleep in the living room watching television. Similarly, when my dad said wake up for school or on weekends, you simply did it. In both cases, if my dad caught you sleeping in the living room late at night or you did not respond to his morning requests to get out of bed, you became the winner of the wet t-shirt contest. My dad would grab the cold water pitcher from the refrigerator and douse you with it. No words. No lashing. No reprimand. You got the message. Whippings weren't really his thing. Of course, he administered a few epic ones in his day, but I think he liked to think of comical punishments. He seemed to get great joy and entertainment from this type of stuff. He humored himself through these punishments. I don't recall him using terminology such as "because I said so" or "just do what I said." Through all of his repercussion tactics, he sent a strong message through swift and high impact action that his words were law and understanding the rules was not a prerequisite for getting the job done.

I was pretty inquisitive as a child. I asked a lot of questions and questioned everything...probably too much. My dad had a signature statement when I questioned him too much, at the wrong time or about the wrong topics. It was: "Don't worry about the horse being blind just load the f#$%&* wagon." Sometimes, actually many times, there were some expletives sprinkled in there before, in the middle, at the end or all of the aforementioned for emphasis to let me know the degree of how hard I should push the process. I began to learn (1) When people tell me to do something, do it first then ask questions, (2) Sometimes, people just want me to do...not think and (3) There may be a bigger scope in play I am unaware of. It took me until I was on my real job out of college to totally understand the nuances in my dad's analogy. I was frustrated on the job. Of course, I thought I knew everything like most young adults in their early 20s. I was talking to my dad about the job and some of its challenges. His response, "Son, sometimes you can't worry about the horse being blind. You just have to load the wagon." It did not take much for me to get it. The youngest of five and living all those years it was then, at that exact moment, it clicked. I totally understood all those years of his rules, order, structure and system. When I am leading and following, I still use this terminology and philosophy.

MY DAD AND ME

IF YOU WANT TO WIN THE KENTUCKY DERBY, SHOW UP WITH A THOROUGHBRED NOT A JACKASS

As a teen, one day I visibly was pissed off at one of my friends. My dad asked me what was wrong. I explained that I had a plan that involved teamwork and one of my friends did not deliver on his promise. My dad asked for clarity with respect to what I asked this friend to do in the grand scheme of the plan. My pops had known my friend for over 10+ years. After I explained the plan, everyone's role and what task I asked my friend to do, my dad questioned, "You asked him to do that?" The comment was his trademark sarcastic line of questioning. After which, he chuckled and then said, "Son, if you want to win the Kentucky Derby, you have to show up with a thoroughbred...not a jackass." In essence, he shared that I created my problem. He helped me realize that there was no way my friend could have delivered. He may have had the best intentions, but his capabilities, effort and resourcefulness would never have delivered what I needed. My dad coached me up on assigning responsibilities, evaluating talent, being 'real' about who can do what, depending on assumptions and hoping for a tiger to miraculously change its stripes.

I am infatuated with the thoroughbred concept that my dad seeded within me. In my personal and professional life, I seek to align myself with thoroughbreds. I gravitate toward individuals, groups, causes and initiatives that are the finest in the pursuit of excellence. I use my dad's words to make sure that the people around me are currently and/or striving to be 'thoroughbreds'. Meaning, one has to be building their mind, body, soul and spirit for a purpose. One must have a race to win. One must be driven psychologically, emotionally and mentally to 'be' a thoroughbred and a winner. Being the youngest boy in the family along with a strong patriarchal overtone in the household, I clung to working hard to outperform the men in the family, on the block and in the neighborhood. I knew that in order to keep up, I had to be a thoroughbred. One of the few family games we had for decades was a ping pong table. I was routinely thrashed by my dad and brothers when they came to visit. My dad would win and tease me. He rigged the ping pong table where it would contort into a 90 degree angle. This enabled me to practice, practice, practice. From my teen years on, my ping pong game was fierce. My skills definitely came in handy during the considerable amount of time I spent in China. As a child, one day I ran to my pops complaining about my youngest big brother terrorizing me, which was regular. My dad simply said, "Don't get mad. Get even." He gave me an idea. Wet him with the water hose when he least expects it. I did it. My dad tricked me. My brother beat me. My dad's response as he was laughing at the whole situation, "You have to run faster, get stronger or be smarter next time." If a problem, shortcoming, failure or anything negative would arise around 2145 or in my adult life, my dad's advice or remedy would ALWAYS be for me to be a thoroughbred. Train like a thoroughbred. Run fast like a thoroughbred. Win the race. Simply be better.

ALWAYS 100% SUPPORT

Hot water can harden an amoebic egg yolk or soften the hardest potato. My dad was like the hot water that hardened my yolk, mind, heart and soul. His fathering was built around being YOUR best...period. He saw every opportunity as a time to post your personal best. My dad spoke of possibilities and never limitations. He simply did not allow for that. Whenever there was a shortcoming, challenge or doubt, he filled that space with encouragement, resources, tools or whatever was needed to remove barriers to excel. When I was in little league, I asked my dad for a bat so I could practice more. He bought it. I became an excellent hitter through little league and high school. When I was 15 years old, I had a summer internship 20 miles from my house. The bus route was treacherous. I started this internship 6 weeks before I was to turn 16 years old and could receive my license. My dad allowed me to drive the car and take the streets. To save time, against my dad's mandate, I used the freeway regularly at age 15. So not only was I driving without a license, I was driving on the freeway. My dad was betting on me big time. I ended up getting into an accident as I ran into the back bumper of a car. The most painful conversation I have ever had with my dad was telling him about the accident. He gritted his teeth, told me how kids that do not listen to their parents fail, and for me not to tell my mother. However, he did not take away my driving privileges. I was able to have a great summer that sparked many of my achievements. When I was preparing to leave for my freshman year in college, my pops bought me an electric typewriter. He did not know too much about my overall needs but he knew I needed a 'weapon' to excel, advance and win. My pops would always provide me, the family, friends, neighbors with resources, help, assistance and support to 'win'.

If there is one all-time empowering memory I have of my dad, it was on my 8th birthday. It will forever rank this day as my single best birthday memory ever. I have had many great moments that I can recall as a child, teen, young adult and grown man, but my 8th birthday is head and shoulders above them all. Not only was it a great day, a momentous day (hey, I was 8) but my pops totally created it. The day started out with a few kids in the backyard for a minor celebration. My dad was barbecuing hot dogs and hamburgers. Moms had the cake in the oven. The small group of kids played, the adults talked, we ate then we had cake and ice cream in the backyard. We sang the birthday song. We went back to playing. Then, that's when the party started! In a flash, my dad and his good friend Earl (I loved Earl too) scooped up the kids. My dad was rolling in his station wagon and Earl had a van. The kids piled into each vehicle. It was all the children, my dad, Earl and a few of my dad's friends who met us at the various stops. We went to the park, then stopped by a parking lot carnival, then to the Big Slide (Note: The Big Slide was a huge slide maybe 2-3 stories high. You climbed up and used a burlap bag to slide down with), then to ride go-carts, then we went to the pizza parlor to eat and finished the day at the airport watching the airplanes fly in above our heads. This was a time before mobile phones and social media, and I am pretty sure my dad or one of the men were

MY DAD AND ME

calling and checking in. When we returned back on the block, all the neighborhood mothers of all the children that came were in front of my house. They were fuming. My dad was cussed out by Earl's wife Ruth. All the kids were quiet. The situation was so tense, I actually thought I did something wrong but I was just along for the ride. My dad played it cool and didn't say a word. It was like a Mexican standoff. Then, my dad made his move. He started singing the birthday song. The kids joined in too. Our energy beat their energy. That was my last memory of that night regardless of the scolding or blowback my dad received from my moms or the neighborhood mothers. There has never been a better night's sleep than the slumber I had that night. It was the first of many moments that my dad 'sold out' for me. My dad was my #1 supporter. I cannot recall a time he ever discouraged me from any idea I had or questioned my decisions. And, I think he was that supportive person to many people. He had impeccable discernment. If it were 3am in the morning and I called my dad and said I need you, he would simply say "I'm on my way." (my moms would too but she would ask at least 3 to 4 questions before she told me she was en route). The most difficult part of life now is that there is no one like him that I can talk to that would listen, analyze and figure out my concern with the intent of my greater good while applying love, encouragement, possibility and absolutely no judgment.

PERFECTLY IMPERFECT

My life has been far from perfect, but I am the perfect son and my dad the perfect dad. There were Robert Lee's Rules of Order but things often were disorderly, unorganized and stuff happened. No s@#$ happened! I remember breaking the biggest window in the house one night. My dad had a golf club behind a door and I started swinging it. I swung the golf club out of my hand and right through the window in the living room. It was one of those 'aww s@#$', I'm in trouble moments. Every type of punishment ran through my mind. When my pops came into the room and said, "What happened?" I came clean and told him exactly what happened. His response, "I knew I should have changed the grip on that club. We will fix it tomorrow. You lucky you didn't hit your momma's lamp." That was my pops right there. S@#$ happens. Roll with the punches. Figure out what needs to happen now, and keep your eye on what you need to do moving forward.

Emotionally, life is tough these days without my dad. I miss him each and every day. There is so much in my day-to-day life, the environment and various scenarios that remind me of him. Some of these thoughts and moments make me laugh and cry, but not such that I am one bit unhappy, remorseful or the like. I am the pinnacle representation of the best that my father had to offer this world. He was truly extraordinary in an ordinary type of way. And, I actually do not wish for my dad to rest in peace. Give 'em hell in heaven, Dad!

CHAPTER TAKEAWAYS

The Book of DH is a series of recollections and pivotal life moments meant to guide any reader who is an aspiring entrepreneur, business professional, or someone simply looking to change their life. Each chapter discusses the experiences and life lessons of Damon Haley, a marketing and business expert, so that you can soar over the hurdles of systems, isms, and privilege in life and business. These takeaways hold his advice and motivation for pursuing a life built on dreams and hopes.

1 | Getting Punched in the Mouth

- Maintain the mindset to compete at all times. Not fight, per se, but always be ready to 'flip the switch' if necessary.

- Others may 'negotiate' fights and conflicts for you. Don't fall into those traps. Pick your own battles and wars.

- Don't think too long and hard over punches, fights and losses. Stuff happens. Learn and move on.

2 | A Monster Stole the Fear

- Don't let fear rule you. Fear is a natural feeling but do not dwell on it. Face it. Conquer it. By doing so, you make better decisions.

- Focus on *why* uncomfortable situations and people vex you and learn the source of the negativity you're feeling. Oftentimes, it is not the person or situation, it is a predisposition that you must evolve from.

- Do not let others use fear as a way to control you. It is a simple dynamic that many people utilize because it is easy to instill fear in others. When you get comfortable with yourself and your decisions, eliminate fear from their arsenal against you.

CHAPTER TAKEAWAYS

3 | Rosa was on to Something

- There may come a time when the system will not be a good fit. Nevertheless, you will always be expected to perform. Quickly figure out a strategy to navigate the system and perform at your highest level until you can move on.

- Always find your champion. Align with that one person (or team) who truly believes in you and who will help you get through challenges.

- Believe in yourself. Don't let any person, scenario or negative vibe stop you. Keep pushing, driving and excelling. Be proud. Be resilient. Be a winner.

4 | Look to the Left, Look to the Right

- Always believe and bet on yourself. Don't compromise who you are and what you stand for. You have been built up and crafted to be who you are with the life experience you have gained. Don't start over for anyone or anything, unless *you* want to improve yourself.

- Remember that it is not quitting if you 'get out' while you are ahead. Sometimes, you have to jump before the end of the ride. Sometimes the driver(s) will not take you where you need to go.

- When you know you are in someone's game, do not get emotional. Learn the rules, understand how to win, game plan, and execute the win.

5 | Wrong Time. Wrong Situation. Wrong Guy.

- When you are in a fiercely competitive environment, you must be highly qualified along with having a little something extra in terms of style, experience or charisma. And, sometimes, the qualifications don't matter because the key decision makers prefer the 'something extra'. Keep it moving, as this is not always the case.

- It gets really tricky at major institutions and in Corporate America. Always seek out truth tellers. You might not like what you hear, but at least you know the facts that make up the story. Over time, you will appreciate the truth.

- Sometimes the grass is greener on the other side. Constantly have real talks with yourself in terms of what you will accept, tolerate and choose to deal with

CHAPTER TAKEAWAYS

in work and in life. At times, you simply reach your limit and must move on. Other times, you may choose to endure. Above all, make it your choice.

6 | The Swoosh Life

- Brands are different from businesses. Don't be fooled, lured or misguided by consumer-facing campaigns, marketing and advertising. Study leadership and how those people operate, which will indicate how you will be measured, promoted and advanced while working on such campaigns.

- Use your position to advance yourself. Do not simply do the work, do you! Your position should be an exchange where you are giving your skills and learning or gaining something in return. If you get hired, then allow all of your talents, gifts and abilities to be on full display. Not for them, but for you.

- Always make note of what is hot and what is not. Do not find yourself working on irrelevant projects, tasks or the like. Be in the epicenter of critical and vital work within your group, business, company, etc. to stay on top of your craft.

7 | The U

- If powerful, influential people provide you with an audience, take full advantage of it. Mesmerize them with your intellect, talents and gifts. More importantly, engage them in a manner where you stand to learn from them as well.

- Take chances on yourself and find others who are risk takers. Risk takers are the people who change the world. Be one of those people. Jobs are cool but adventures are better.

- Build a team and a system that is built to last. Secure the most talented and creative people to lead your charge. Always do groundbreaking work and don't settle for less.

8 | Mr. International

- Test your limits physically, geographically, mentally and culturally. Earth is a big place. You grow exponentially when you experience other cultures, places and ways of doing things. Don't just Google it. Go see it.

CHAPTER TAKEAWAYS

- In order to perform at a high level you must steady your mind. It is tough to do this with the systems, isms and privileges always at work. If you can block out the psychological noise at key moments when you need to rise up, you will have phenomenal success.

- Life is different for black folks outside of the United States, it's worth experiencing different sides of yourself abroad. Trust me.

9 | Nothing Lasts Forever

- In the service business, unless you have an undeniable bundle of talent or you are integrated into the corporate leadership structure, you will face the end of the relationship at some point. Diversify your client list and always plan an exit or transition strategy.

- If you love an industry, exhaust every resource you can to remain a part of it before you decide to make a transition.

- Remember, it is business...not personal. Knowing this will help you stay unbothered by external conditions, no matter what happens.

10 | Hold Up, the Party is Not Over

- Develop and cultivate your transferable skills. Keep a running tab of how many tools you have and can utilize. If all you have is a hammer, then act as if everything is a nail. Stay overqualified to do it all.

- Don't be boxed in. Believe that you have the power to succeed in anything you choose to do in life. Don't stop, won't stop, can't stop should be a part of your mindset.

- If you claim to be about business, buy one, buy two, or own a few. In the end, if the businesses are successful you can then do whatever you want to do!

DH READING LIST

Sun Tzu's The Art of War Plus The Warrior Class: 306 Lessons in Strategy
by Gary Gagliardi and Sun Tzu

Becoming a Person of Influence: How to Positively Impact the Lives of Others
by John Maxwell

Building Left-Brain Power: Left-Brain Conditioning Exercises and Tips to Strengthen Language, Math and Uniquely Human Skills
by Allen Bragdon and David Gamon

Codes, Ciphers and Secret Writing
by Martin Gardner

Confessions of an Economic Hit Man
by John Perkins

The Dip: A Little Book That Teaches You When to Quit (and When to Stick)
by Seth Godin

Extreme Ownership: How U.S. Navy SEALs Lead and Win
by Jocko Willink and Leif Babin

The Four Agreements: A Practical Guide to Personal Freedom
by Don Miguel Ruiz

The Full Armor of God
by Larry Richards

The Head Game: High-Efficiency Analytic Decision-Making and the Art of Solving Complex Problems Quickly
by Philip Mudd

DH READING LIST

The Hero with a Thousand Faces
by Joseph Campbell

How Successful People Think: Change Your Thinking, Change Your Life
by John Maxwell

Invisible Man
by Ralph Ellison

The Master Key System
by Charles F. Haanel

Monster: The Autobiography of an L.A. Gang Member
by Sanyika Shakur

The Perfect Kill: 21 Laws for Assassins
by Robert Baer

Permission Marketing: Turning Strangers Into Friends and Friends Into Customers
by Seth Godin

Pimp: The Story of My Life
by Iceberg Slim

The Power of Your Other Hand: Unlock Creativity and Inner Wisdom Through the Right Side of Your Brain
by Lucia Capacchione

Psycho-Cybernetics
by Maxwell Maltz

Quadrivium: The Four Classical Liberal Arts of Number, Geometry, Music, & Cosmology
by Miranda Lundy & Anthony Ashton

The Servant Leader
by Ken Blanchard & Phil Hodges